Superpowers

The USA
The USSR

Imperial Visions
The Rise and Fall of Empires

Superpowers

The USA

The USSR

Max M. Mintz
The USA

John Bennet
The USSR

Preface by Bayrd Still
Professor Emeritus of History
New York University

HBJ Press
a subsidiary of Harcourt Brace Jovanovich
New York, New York

HBJ Press

Publisher, John R. Whitman
Executive Editor, Marcia Heath
Managing Editor, Janice Lemmo
Series Editors: John Radziewicz, Suzanne Stewart
Editorial Production: Hope Keller, Warren B. Scharf

Marketing Staff: Mark A. Mayer, Ken Santor, Jose J. Elizalde, Laurie Farber, Nancy Ryan

Authors: Max M. Mintz, John Bennet
Picture Researcher, Janet Adams

Consultants
   The USA: Professor Bayrd Still
   The USSR: Professor James Miller

Design Implementation, Designworks

Rizzoli Editore

Authors of the Italian Edition
   Introduction: Professor Ovidio Dallera
   The USA: Dr. Massimo Fini
   The USSR: Professor Ugo Basso
   Maps: Gian Franco Leonardi
Idea and Realization, Harry C. Lindinger
Graphic Design, Gerry Valsecchi
General Editorial Supervisor, Ovidio Dallera

© 1980 Rizzoli Editore
Printed in Italy.

Library of Congress Cataloging in Publication Data

Mintz, Max M.
   Superpowers, the USA, the USSR.

   (Imperial visions; 12)
   Includes index.
   1. United States—History. 2. Russia—History—
20th century. I. Bennet, John, 1945—joint author
II. Title III. Series
E178.M675   947.084   79-2530
ISBN 0-15-004035-0

Contents

Preface   7

The USA   9

Franklin—The quintessential American?   24
The sage of Monticello   36
The Louisiana Purchase   38
The persuaders   46
The Plains Indian   54
The iron horse   58
Gold rush   72
The inventor-promoter   78
The new immigrants   82

The USSR   89

1905: "Dress rehearsal" for 1917   98
Vladimir Ilyich Lenin   112
Leon Trotsky   127
The Kremlin   135
Electrification   138
Poet of the Revolution   142
Soviet art   150
The USSR   154
The purges   157
Sergei Eisenstein   158
Propaganda   162

Photography Credits   170
Index   171

Preface

The USA and the USSR are the offspring of revolutions, and for both, the ideals of their revolutions have justified territorial expansion. Unlike the old European colonial empires with possessions scattered around the globe, today's two superpowers are geographically compact and measure their world-wide influence in terms of allies. Only in their increasingly restive borderlands have the superpowers sought to exert traditional dominion over neighboring states.

In a world dominated by monarchies, the American Revolution (1775–1783) brought forth a self-confident republic that fervently proclaimed its "mission" and "manifest destiny" to extend constitutional government from sea to sea, dislodging and forcibly relocating the aboriginal inhabitants and, by war or diplomacy, removing any nation that stood in its way. Population growth, immigration, and revolutions in transportation and technology all helped impel American expansion to the Pacific, and land-hungry farmers as well as businessmen eager to exploit the continent's seemingly limitless resources joined in equating territorial growth with the national good. The drive westward was thus a response to the nation's individualistic, republican ideology.

By contrast, the Soviet Union was created as a means of giving a new unity to vast territories and dozens of peoples already brought together during centuries of autocratic rule. After czarist Russia's collapse in 1917, the Bolsheviks, under the masterful leadership of Lenin and Trotsky, managed to impose a new, Marxist order on what came to be known as the Union of Soviet Socialist Republics. Like the USA, the USSR was a federation capable of expanding through the absorption of new members; like the USA, the USSR proclaimed itself the embodiment of human destiny. But while in the USA the underlying principle has been that government should permit the play of competing interests and should protect the individual's civil rights, the rulers of the USSR have maintained that history is the battleground between hostile classes and, further, that abstract human rights are hollow bourgeois shams.

A clash of interests between the USA and the USSR was perhaps inevitable. In a single decade, the 1930s, Soviet Russia was transformed from an agrarian society with a modest industrial base into a major power by mobilizing its economic potential through ruthless centralization. After Germany's defeat in World War Two, when the Soviet Union moved into formerly German-dominated Eastern Europe, the brutality with which Stalin asserted Soviet authority from Poland to Bulgaria prompted profound apprehension in the United States—the rival superpower that had emerged from the war. The westward reach of what was soon called the Iron Curtain convinced Americans that the USSR was not simply achieving its age-old goal of securing its borderlands against new invaders but rather that Stalin had made his first moves in a campaign to spread Communism throughout the world. Revolution in China seemed to confirm the danger. It was not long before the United States came to see itself as the champion of the capitalist democracies in the struggle against the Soviet Union and Communism.

By 1949 the United States reversed its long-held policy of avoiding permanent foreign "entanglements," joining eleven other nations in the anti-Soviet NATO alliance. Similar pacts were later forged in Asia and Latin America. The threat of nuclear warfare, menacing human survival since 1945, helped prevent a direct military conflict between the superpowers, which tirelessly raced against each other for influence among the new nations emerging from colonialism in Africa and elsewhere.

The 1970s brought additional complexities to Soviet-American relations. Despite immense natural wealth and awesome military capabilities, both superpowers had to recognize the emergent influence of hitherto more acquiescent allies, and both learned painful lessons about limits of growth and power. Common ideology could not avert open hostility between China and the Soviet Union. Yugoslavia and Cuba defied their giant neighbors. Western Europe, Japan, and several OPEC nations surpassed the United States in certain crucial economic and technological areas. The developing nations demanded control of their own resources and destinies, and events in Vietnam, Iran, and Afghanistan cast doubt upon the superpowers' ability to retain control of Third World nations bent upon their own self-advancement. Whether the very concept of two superpowers astride the world will endure—and to what extent their original ideological precepts will continue to define Soviet and American "missions"—the last two decades of the twentieth century will no doubt tell.

BAYRD STILL
Professor Emeritus of History
New York University

The USA

"We have it in our power to begin the world over again," declared the Revolutionary pamphleteer Thomas Paine in 1776. Ever since 1492, when Christopher Columbus was grandly commissioned "Admiral of the Ocean Sea," Americans have had lofty ambitions. The Puritans of Massachusetts Bay strove to found a utopian Biblical "City on a Hill"; the settlers on the frontier hoped to establish a pure democracy; and twentieth-century crusading reformers launched a fervent campaign for social justice. Much was achieved, but much remained unrealized. For white northern Europeans seeking upward mobility, refuge

from religious persecution, or escape from poverty and even prison, America provided opportunity. For African blacks, manacled into slavery and shipped indiscriminately across the Atlantic, America was a land of humiliation. And for many southern and eastern Europeans, America meant slum tenements and second-class citizenship. Yet, despite its short-comings, America symbolized a "New World," a land of inexhaustible resources and endless promise.

The intermingling of the immigrants and their response to the environment spawned a new personality. The new man with the "west-bred face," the American poet Walt Whitman proclaimed, "never knew how it felt to stand in the presence of superiors." Rarely, at least, in the presence of titled aristocrats, who usually preferred to stay home on their ancestral lands. New fortunes might be made, and few impoverished immigrants needed to despair of earning a competence. In the rush to carve new communities, old habits and ideas were often modified or discarded. Just as the horizon seemed boundless, so any venture seemed possible.

The American became, or saw himself as, an enterprising experimenter, a self-reliant jack-of-all-trades ever ready to begin life anew. Heedless of the past and preoccupied with the future, he would not be denied. If Indian tribes resisted westward migration, they were dispossessed by war or treaty and later herded onto reservations. In the South, as white farm laborers became scarce or too expensive, slaves were imported as substitutes. The conquest of a virgin domain was not an undertaking for gentle sensibilities. Yet the same harsh struggle generated a code of fair play and respect for the individual.

Ability became more important than blood, class, or place of birth. The Declaration of Independence had little choice but to pronounce all men equal, not just Englishmen. Ultimately, that meant blacks as well as whites, even if it required a civil war, fought some ninety years later, to excise the canker of slav-

For the millions of immigrants who have been part of what is widely recognized as the greatest population movement in history, New York City has been the gateway to the New World. The Statue of Liberty (preceding page), with Emma Lazarus' welcome on its base to the "huddled masses yearning to breathe free," lifts its torch three hundred feet high above New York harbor. Sculpted by Frédéric Bartholdi, it was unveiled in 1886 as a gift from the French people, paid for by thousands of private contributions.

Facing page, top to bottom, aerial views depicting East Coast terrain much as it appeared when the first colonists arrived: a Pennsylvania stretch of the Appalachian Mountains, revealing the typical parallel ridge pattern that facilitated north-south travel but temporarily retarded westward migration; hilly Connecticut woods in autumn; and Nantucket Sound, as seen from Martha's Vineyard. Above, upstate New York lake country, near Grahamsville, in the Catskill Mountains. Right, the characteristically rocky Maine coast. The Delaware River (below) in part separates New Jersey from Pennsylvania, Pennsylvania from New York, and New Jersey from Delaware.

Top, a Seneca Indian mask made of corn husks. The Seneca belonged to the upstate New York League of the Iroquois. The Indians adapted the white man's materials, as in the Iroquois silver inlaid tomahawk (above left), used both as a weapon and a work tool. Above center, a beaded knife sheath. Immediately above, a woven turkey effigy in the tradition of early American folk art.

The French exploratory challenge to the British in North America was led by Jacques Cartier. He landed at Labrador (center) in northeastern Canada in 1534 and returned in 1535 and 1541. Sailing up the St. Lawrence River to Montreal, he engaged in fruitless searches for a northwest passage to the Pacific and for the mythical Indian kingdom of Saguenay.

ery. And, although there were those who would deny complete equality ("Besides," asked Whitman, "is not America for the Whites? And is it not better so?"), and the road would be slow and laden with barriers, the future would bring advances in racial justice.

The Americans built an empire on a radically new principle: the admission of territories to the Union as new states on a basis of equality with the old. Almost without exception, previous empires had used their holdings for tribute or profit. In America, the continent was to be treated as a shared possession, to be peopled by compatriots, not colonists. And the new democracy, ardent expansionists preached, was

The first permanent British settlement in the New World was established at Jamestown, Virginia, on May 13, 1607. Above, landing parties on the James River. The colonists soon discovered a substitute for the gold they had been seeking—tobacco.

Romanticized accounts credit the English courtier Sir Walter Raleigh (below) with naming Virginia after Queen Elizabeth, the Virgin Queen; in reality, it was the queen's idea to name the colony after herself.

"manifestly destined" to reach from the Atlantic to the Pacific—even, perhaps, to encompass the entire continent. It was, a Jacksonian journalist asserted in 1845, "the simple solid weight" of millions of advancing Americans.

The settlers pushed westward, enticed by soil "of the blackness of ink" and "nature's greatest lottery scheme"—gold fever. To keep pace with them, lands were purchased or wrested not only from Britain, but from France, Spain, Mexico, and Russia. The Civil War momentarily threatened to halt the advance, but after General Robert E. Lee surrendered to General Ulysses S. Grant at Appomattox the reunited

nation raced forward with renewed vigor. By 1890, the Census Bureau announced that the west was won: A continuous unsettled wilderness no longer existed.

The habit of expansion inspired a venture in overseas imperialism—what diplomatic historian Samuel Flagg Bemis called "The Great Aberration of 1898," but it soon subsided. Although Americans voiced an early interest in foreign trade outlets, they were too busy exploiting the plentiful resources of their own continent to heed Rudyard Kipling's injunction to "take up the white man's burden." Of the new foreign territorial acquisitions, the Philippines were freed in 1946 and Hawaii became a state in 1959. The

Commonwealth of Puerto Rico will soon determine its own future.

The key to the emergence of the United States as a world power was its development of a business civilization. The nineteenth-century commentator Alexis de Tocqueville, in searching for clues to the American character, accosted a sailor on the street: "I inquire why the ships of his country are built so as to last but for a short time; he answers without hesitation that the art of navigation is every day making such rapid progress that the finest vessel would become almost useless if it lasted beyond a certain number of years." In these words, falling "accidentally and on a partic-

ular subject from a man of rude attainments," Tocqueville sensed "the general and systematic idea upon which a great people directs all its concerns." The plenitude and the sheer immensity of America inspired profligate, yet daring, innovation. The American businessman, his eye fixed inexorably on the profit and loss balance sheet, did not hesitate to scrap an outdated steam engine, family farm, town mansion, or city business block even if they functioned efficiently.

Big business promoted big enterprise. After 1865, with the subjugation of the agricultural South, the way was paved for the construction of transcontinen-

tal railroads, the consolidation of steel and oil production, and the increase in the number of large urban centers. Standardized products, mass manufacture, and mass marketing vastly increased production and consumption. Farms were mechanized and commercialized to feed the burgeoning population. The general standard of living rose to a level higher than anywhere else in the world.

By the twentieth century, the new affluence brought with it a new internationalism. The American economy required vital foreign raw materials and overseas markets and avenues for investment. American military power could make the difference in any major armed struggle. The possibility of global destruction joined the United States with the other nations of the world in a bond of shared vulnerability.

From the Gulf of Mexico a branch of the Gulf Stream, the warm Azores Current, flows eastward across the Atlantic. Helped along by friendly winds, it skirts the Azores, an island chain situated 800 miles west of the European mainland and belonging to Portugal. It was on these islands, in the fifteenth century, that local inhabitants came upon collections of strange objects cast along the shores: primitive artifacts, branches of an unknown species of tree, and the

Oxford-educated William Penn negotiated treaties with the Indians (above) for land titles to his Quaker colony at Philadelphia. Despotic Peter Stuyvesant (below left), the last Dutch governor of New Netherland Colony (later New York), unsuccessfully re- *sisted the British takeover in 1664. Peter Minuit, who in 1626 purchased Manhattan Island from the Indians for twenty-four dollars' worth of trinkets, also negotiated a purchase west of the Hudson in 1631 (immediately below).*

The Pilgrim ship Mayflower *(above), carrying 102 passengers, came within sight of Cape Cod on November 9, 1620. Although the Pilgrims had intended to settle farther south, they disembarked at Plymouth (far left) on Christmas Day. One of the first buildings erected was a blockhouse similar to the one (near left) in today's reconstructed Pilgrim Village. Plymouth was absorbed in 1691 by Massachusetts Bay Colony.*

The first British acquisition in the French and Indian War was the Canadian port of Louisbourg (near right) on July 26, 1758. There, land and sea forces under General Jeffrey Amherst and Admiral Edward Boscawen won control of the entrance to the St. Lawrence River. The war became a contest for the Ohio Valley, into which Anglo-American frontiersmen like Daniel Boone (below right) were soon advancing.

bodies of two men with broad, non-European faces. Listening to reports of these findings from his home in the nearby Madeira Islands was Christopher Columbus, a seasoned Genoese sailor but an incompetent geographer. Enormously self-confident and imbued with religious zeal, he persuaded King Ferdinand and Queen Isabella of Spain in 1492 to authorize a voyage to the Indies, which he asserted were only 3,000 miles distant. Navigating with unreliable instruments and quelling a near mutiny, he landed in the Bahamas on October 12 and never doubted that he had reached the Indies.

Much to the dislike of Ferdinand and Isabella, Spain was soon joined by England in the race to stake New World claims. Over the protest of the Spanish ambassador, King Henry VII commissioned John Cabot—like Columbus, a Genoese navigator—to discover and acquire lands in the New World. Cabot's voyages (1497 and 1498) and the explorations of his son Sebastian formed the basis for England's later assertion of titled claims to the eastern coast of the present-day United States.

This northern continent, John Cabot reported, was "a very good and temperate country," but from the cold reaches of Maine to the steamy swamps of Florida it presented a thick, rarely interrupted mantle of forest. The Appalachian Mountains, another formidable barrier, also impeded westward migration. These obstacles, as it turned out, proved blessings in disguise, for they prevented the colonists from dissipating their energies as previous settlers had done. The Spaniards, once established in Mexico, ineffectually fanned out into what is now the American Southwest. The French, drawn rapidly into the interior by the St. Lawrence River and the Great Lakes, exhausted their strength in the continental expanse. The Americans, however, spent their first hundred and fifty years consolidating their settlements east of the Appalachians. When they finally crossed the mountains they were numerous and strong enough to drive out all contenders before them.

Settlement of the Mississippi River Valley acted as

The dashing young general James Wolfe lost his life (top right) during his masterly capture of Quebec from the French on September 18, 1759. The fall of Montreal a year later ended the war in America. Later, during the Revolution, the British fought the Americans for the Ohio Territory, with the aid of the Iroquois Indians (above right). In 1778, George Rogers Clark (near right) led a band of rangers through the wilderness to defeat the British at the Mississippi River settlements of Kaskaskia and Cahokia. His victories secured the Illinois country, which had first been explored by the French Jesuit missionary Jacques (Père) Marquette and the fur trader Louis Joliet (below) in the spring of 1673.

a powerful force for nationalization. Within this area northerners and southerners mixed freely and developed a common, rooted identity. Ultimately the lure of land and gold carried them across the Great Plains (thought to be a vast desert) and over the Rocky Mountains to the Pacific.

The "Indians" the colonists encountered were racially akin to people of a Mongoloid type who had crossed the Bering Strait from Asia to Alaska probably before 10,000 B.C. They numbered almost a million for the entire area that was to become the United States and Canada. Living in a subsistence economy, the Indians had no conception of private property

The Stamp Act, requiring taxation of all American official documents and printed matter, was unpopular even in England. In this British cartoon (left) of March 18, 1766, the act's author, George Grenville, participates in its funeral. Above, the uncompromising King George III, who insisted on the act's legality. Tension between colonists and British soldiers provoked the Boston Massacre (right) on March 5, 1770; five colonists were killed in self-defense by British troops.

The Marquis de Lafayette (left) volunteered for the American cause at the age of nineteen. Paul Revere (above), a Boston silversmith, alerted the patriots to the British march on Concord. "No man," declared George Washington (right) in 1769, should "hesitate a moment to use arms" in defense of American freedom.

and were at first willing to share their hunting grounds with the Europeans. Only when they discovered that they were allowing themselves to be dispossessed did outright conflict erupt. The Indians were fierce in their attacks on the settlers, and the whites, for their part, were unsparing to the point of exterminating whole populations. The slaughter constitutes one of the most tragic chapters in American history.

The first successful British settlement in America took root at Jamestown, Virginia. The Virginia Company of London, licensed by Queen Elizabeth I to populate the southern Atlantic coast, dispatched three ships in December 1607 which four months later arrived at Chesapeake Bay. The site chosen for colonization, thirty miles up the James River, was originally thought to be an ideal, secluded setting. The rigors of the swampy and mosquito-infested terrain, a lack of fresh water, and the ever-present threat of attack by the Indians, however, all confirmed the flaws in their choice. The shortsightedness of the colonists themselves further hindered the development of the colony. Ill-prepared fortune hunters who spent more time searching for a northwest passage and digging for gold than in constructing houses and clearing

The Tea Act so enraged Bostonians that a revolutionary band called the Sons of Liberty boarded three ships anchored off Griffin's Wharf on December 16, 1773, and cast ninety thousand pounds of tea into the harbor (above).

A British cartoon of October 31, 1774 (right), portrays gleeful Bostonians who have tarred and feathered a customs agent. The victim is being subjected to an additional ignominy: He must gulp a tea toast to each member of the royal family.

farms, the settlers almost doomed Jamestown from the outset.

The emergence of Captain John Smith as the group's leader saved the settlement. A headstrong adventurer who had been jailed for mutiny during the voyage, Smith decreed that "he that will not worke, shall not eate." He made peace with the Indians and began growing maize. Under his successors, tobacco cultivation was introduced, which yielded a cash crop. The Virginia Company, however, received no return on its investment. Its only profit came from a subsidiary that supplied 140 women, "not enforcing them to marrie against their wills," for whom de-

On the afternoon of the Boston Tea Party, seven thousand people gathered at the Old South Meeting House (right). "Boston harbor a tea-pot tonight!" was the cry. Below, Massachusetts Minutemen, who were renowned for their ability to assemble at a moment's notice. On the night of April 18, 1775, Paul Revere and William Dawes sounded an alarm for their services.

lighted potential husbands paid at auction as much as 150 pounds of tobacco per head.

Gradually, class differentiations, which had always existed, became more pronounced. Tobacco cultivation, with its greedy exhaustion of the soil, encouraged the growth of large plantations. "Indentured" (contracted) servants, required to work four to seven years to pay back the cost of their passage from England, provided some of the labor. But shiploads of enslaved blacks from western Africa became the mainstay of the work force. Small farmers of the western piedmont, resentful of domination by tidewater (coastal) planters and critical of inadequate protection against the Indians, in 1676 deposed the governor, massacred two Indian tribes, and burned Jamestown. When their leader, Nathaniel Bacon, Jr., died of dysentery, Governor Sir William Berkeley hanged twenty-three of the rebels—"more men," Charles II angrily exclaimed, "than I have done for the murder of my father."

By the eighteenth century an enclave of patrician families had settled in the "Northern Neck," between the Rappahannock and Potomac rivers, the home of the Carters, Fairfaxes, Washingtons, Madisons, and Monroes. These luxury-loving, status-conscious planters, who never paid a bill "until, like their Madeira, it had acquired age," served as the colonies' local magistrates and members of the House of Burgesses, maintaining a high ethical standard of public service. Similar social systems evolved in Maryland and the Carolinas.

Religion spurred the founding of the northern colonies. The Pilgrims who disembarked from the *Mayflower* at Plymouth Rock in 1620 were Calvinists. After separating from the Church of England, they sought refuge first in Holland and then had obtained the sponsorship of a group of London merchants to settle in the New World. Two thirds of the first shipload, however, were "strangers" (non-Pilgrims), and to insure peace and order male adults were asked to sign the Mayflower Compact, agreeing to "covenant and combine" themselves into a "civil Body Politick" for the purpose of enacting "just and equal Laws." The colony did little more than survive, for it lacked good soil, a good harbor, and a royal charter.

The Puritans of Massachusetts Bay fared better. Willing to remain within the Church of England, they received a charter from Charles I. They initially settled at Salem in 1628 and then spread rapidly to the area around Boston: Within ten years they attracted fifteen to twenty thousand immigrants. In small, industrious communities, they sought to establish models of Christian piety. It was a hard creed, and even among the faithful only one third were granted church membership. "Christ hath his flock," declared the Reverend Thomas Shepard in 1641, "and that is but a little flock." Government was at first closely tied to the church, resting in the hands of Governor John Winthrop and a few magistrates drawn from the rising merchant class. But, under increased popular pressure, nonchurch members were permitted to vote in town meetings, a bicameral legislature was established, and legal codes replaced arbitrary judicial decisions based solely on the Bible.

Relations with the Indians, who had been decimated by a smallpox outbreak in 1617, began peacefully. When the Pequots of Connecticut, however, resisted colonial encroachment in 1637, more than five

Above, the early American flag, "thirteen stripes, alternate red and white" and "thirteen stars, white in a blue field."

Massachusetts militiamen (below) snipe at British troops returning to Charlestown, near Boston, from Concord on April 19, 1775.

BOSTON

hundred of them were slaughtered. In 1675, a haughty Wampanoag chieftain, dubbed "King Philip" by the colonists, led a general uprising in which twelve towns were destroyed and more than a thousand settlers killed. After Philip was shot in the succeeding year, and his wife and child sold into West Indian slavery, the resistance of the Indians of New England was broken.

Massachusetts was the springboard for the rest of the New England colonies. Rhode Island was founded by two exiles: Roger Williams, a preacher who advocated religious freedom, separation of church and state, and respect for the property rights of Indians; and Anne Hutchinson, a believer in intuitive revelation, whom Governor Winthrop characterized as "more bold than a man." Connecticut was formed through the union of two groups from Massachusetts, one under the Reverend Thomas Hooker at Hartford, and the other, an uncompromising Puritan faction under the Reverend John Davenport and Theophilus Eaton, at New Haven. New Hampshire, founded in 1638, was absorbed by Massachusetts but made a separate royal colony in 1680. James II attempted in 1685 to create a combined Dominion of New England under the dictatorial authority of Sir Edmund Andros, but with the overthrow of James in

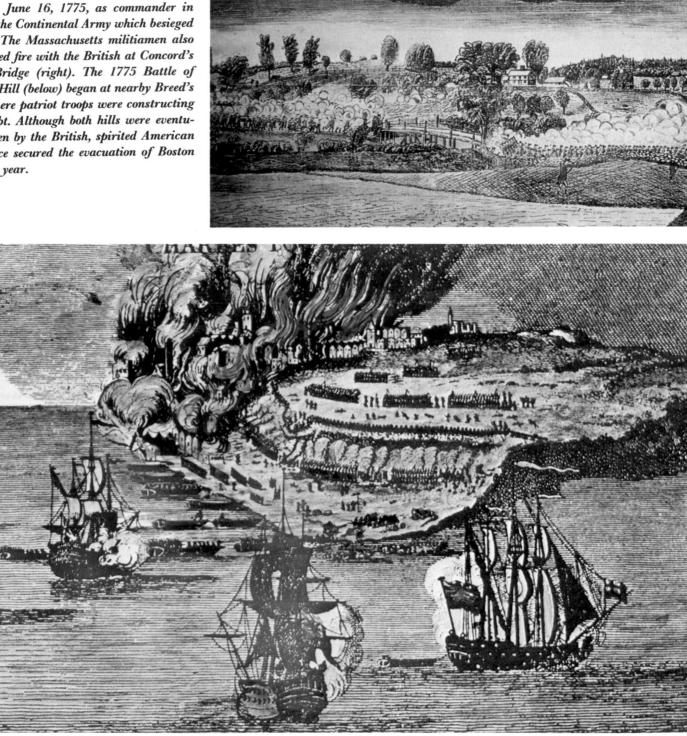

George Washington (left) accepted appointment on June 16, 1775, as commander in chief of the Continental Army which besieged Boston. The Massachusetts militiamen also exchanged fire with the British at Concord's North Bridge (right). The 1775 Battle of Bunker Hill (below) began at nearby Breed's Hill, where patriot troops were constructing a redoubt. Although both hills were eventually taken by the British, spirited American resistance secured the evacuation of Boston the next year.

Franklin–the quintessential American?

Benjamin Franklin achieved many coveted distinctions—as an inventor, businessman, scientist, philosopher, author, statesman, educator, and philanthropist. Retiring at forty-two to devote himself to public service and private enlightenment, Franklin founded a circulating library, a preparatory school, a philosophical society, a hospital, a fire department, and a police force. Although a self-proclaimed moderate who preached thrift and hard work, he pursued life's pleasures to the fullest, particularly during his tenure in London and Paris (his unlettered wife remained in America).

After his nine-year stay in France (1776-1785), where he negotiated an alliance with the French and a peace treaty with the British, he returned to Philadelphia to become one of the signers of the Constitution. Just before his death, Franklin declared that, having been favored with many evidences of divine benevolence in this life, he had "no doubt of its continuance in the next, though without the smallest conceit of meriting such goodness."

Immediately below, a portrait of Benjamin Franklin in middle age. Near right, his foolhardy kite experiment, in June of 1752. Franklin and his illegitimate son, William, might have been killed if the wire on the silk kite had attracted a stronger charge of electricity. The experience inspired his invention of the lightning rod. Below right, a collection of Franklin's letters penned in Paris.

Above, Franklin at work on one of the engravings for his newspaper, the Pennsylvania Gazette. *His cartoon "Join or Die" urged an inter-colonial union.*

Immediately below, some of the laboratory apparatus used to demonstrate the efficacy of the lightning rod. Franklin also invented bifocal eyeglasses.

At age seventeen, Franklin worked in Samuel Keimer's print shop (right). "I made the ink; I was a warehouse man, and everything; in short quite a factotum," he once stated.

Franklin returned from France on September 14, 1785, to a rousing welcome in Philadelphia (left). Two years later, he became a delegate to the Constitutional Convention. Too infirm to take the floor, he asked James Wilson to read his appeal requesting that every member who had objections to the Constitution would, like himself, "doubt a little of his own infallibility" and sign.

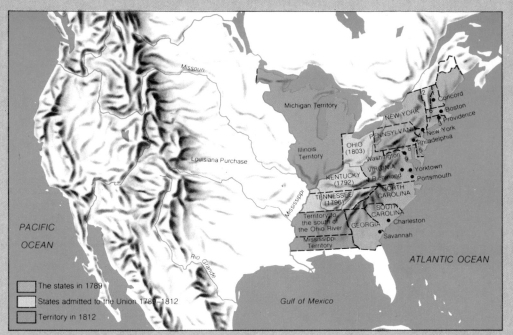

Significant precedents were set during the first thirty years of the American republic for the eventual expansion to the Pacific. The Northwest Ordinance of 1787 established an orderly process for the creation of new states equal in authority to the original thirteen. The purchase of Louisiana in 1803 doubled the national domain and secured for Westerners free access to the mouth of the Mississippi River.

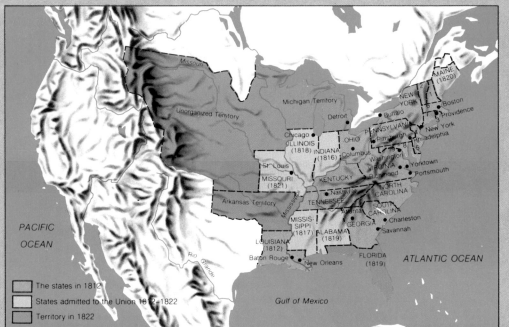

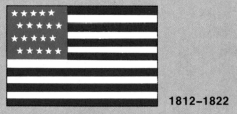

The War of 1812 brought Britain's final acceptance of American independence. In 1818, the two nations agreed on a northern boundary for the Louisiana Territory and the administration of the Oregon country. Florida was purchased from Spain in 1819, and the western boundary of the Louisiana Purchase was clarified. The status of slavery in the territories created a deep North-South rift.

This was an era of internal settlement and territorial expansion. The Maine-Canada boundary was resolved in 1842. Texas was annexed in 1845, and the United States soon gained sole possession of the Oregon country to the 49th parallel. Acquired through the Mexican War were California, New Mexico, and parts of Utah, Nevada, and Arizona. The Gadsden Purchase (1853) added land in the Southwest.

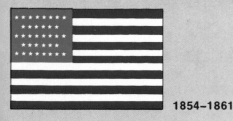

1854–1861

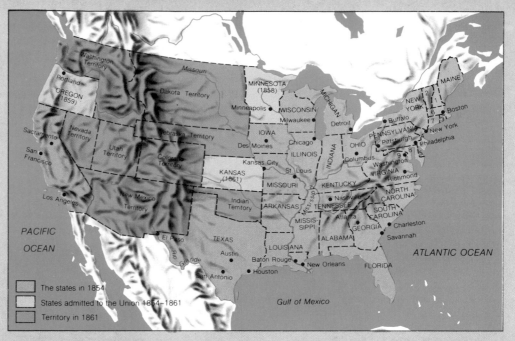

The seven years before 1861 were dominated by a nationwide dispute over whether slavery should exist in the territories: The controversial Kansas-Nebraska Act of 1854 left the decision to each new state. Proslavery and antislavery settlers poured in, each group attempting to outvote the other. The resulting bloodshed and disputed elections delayed the admission of Kansas to the Union until 1861.

The states in 1854
States admitted to the Union 1854–1861
Territory in 1861

1861–1865

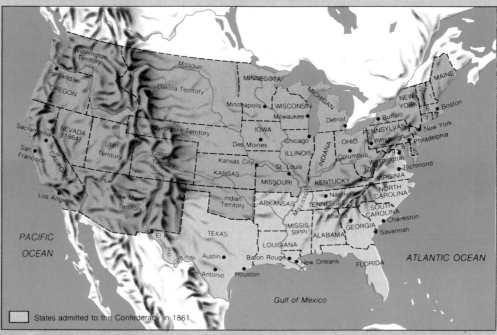

The Civil War determined that America would occupy the expanse between the Atlantic and Pacific as a united nation. General Ulysses S. Grant split the Confederacy vertically by winning control of the Mississippi River and horizontally by sending General William T. Sherman on his march from Tennessee to Georgia. Grant then battered General Robert E. Lee into submission at Richmond.

States admitted to the Confederacy in 1861

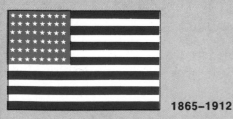

1865–1912

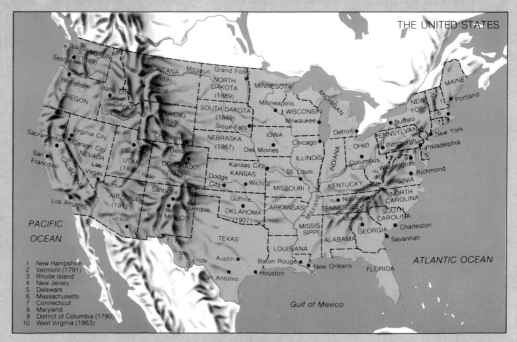

Gold miners, cattlemen, farmers, and city builders figured in the settlement of the West after the Civil War. Transcontinental railroads delivered swarms of settlers from Europe and the East. The Indian was subjugated and sequestered. By 1912, twelve additional states had been created from the remaining western territories, thus completing the organization of the coterminous United States.

1. New Hampshire
2. Vermont (1791)
3. Rhode Island
4. New Jersey
5. Delaware
6. Massachusetts
7. Connecticut
8. Maryland
9. District of Columbia (1790)
10. West Virginia (1863)

IN CONGRESS, JULY 4, 1776.

The unanimous Declaration of the thirteen united States of America,

When in the Course of human events, it becomes necessary for one people to dissolve the political bands which have connected them with another, and to assume among the Powers of the earth, the separate and equal station to which the Laws of Nature and of Nature's God entitle them, a decent respect to the opinions of mankind requires that they should declare the causes which impel them to the separation.

We hold these truths to be self-evident, that all men are created equal, that they are endowed by their Creator with certain unalienable Rights, that among these are Life, Liberty and the pursuit of Happiness.—That to secure these rights, Governments are instituted among Men, deriving their just powers from the consent of the governed,—That whenever any Form of Government becomes destructive of these ends, it is the Right of the People to alter or to abolish it, and to institute new Government, laying its foundation on such principles and organizing its powers in such form, as to them shall seem most likely to effect their Safety and Happiness. Prudence, indeed, will dictate that Governments long established should not be changed for light and transient causes; and accordingly all experience hath shewn, that mankind are more disposed to suffer, while evils are sufferable, than to right themselves by abolishing the forms to which they are accustomed. But when a long train of abuses and usurpations, pursuing invariably the same Object evinces a design to reduce them under absolute Despotism, it is their right, it is their duty, to throw off such Government, and to provide new Guards for their future security.—Such has been the patient sufferance of these Colonies; and such is now the necessity which constrains them to alter their former Systems of Government. The history of the present King of Great Britain is a history of repeated injuries and usurpations, all having in direct object the establishment of an absolute Tyranny over these States. To prove this, let Facts be submitted to a candid world.

He has refused his Assent to Laws, the most wholesome and necessary for the public good.

He has forbidden his Governors to pass Laws of immediate and pressing importance, unless suspended in their operation till his Assent should be obtained; and when so suspended, he has utterly neglected to attend to them.

He has refused to pass other Laws for the accommodation of large districts of people, unless those people would relinquish the right of Representation in the Legislature, a right inestimable to them and formidable to tyrants only.

He has called together legislative bodies at places unusual, uncomfortable, and distant from the depository of their public Records, for the sole purpose of fatiguing them into compliance with his measures.

He has dissolved Representative Houses repeatedly, for opposing with manly firmness his invasions on the rights of the people.

He has refused for a long time, after such dissolutions, to cause others to be elected; whereby the Legislative powers, incapable of Annihilation, have returned to the People at large for their exercise; the State remaining in the mean time exposed to all the dangers of invasion from without, and convulsions within.

He has endeavoured to prevent the population of these States; for that purpose obstructing the Laws for Naturalization of Foreigners; refusing to pass others to encourage their migrations hither, and raising the conditions of new Appropriations of Lands.

He has obstructed the Administration of Justice, by refusing his Assent to Laws for establishing Judiciary powers.

He has made Judges dependent on his Will alone, for the tenure of their offices, and the amount and payment of their salaries.

He has erected a multitude of New Offices, and sent hither swarms of Officers to harrass our people, and eat out their substance.

He has kept among us, in times of peace, Standing Armies without the Consent of our legislatures.

He has affected to render the Military independent of and superior to the Civil power.

He has combined with others to subject us to a jurisdiction foreign to our constitution, and unacknowledged by our laws; giving his Assent to their Acts of pretended Legislation:

For Quartering large bodies of armed troops among us:

For protecting them, by a mock Trial, from punishment for any Murders which they should commit on the Inhabitants of these States:

For cutting off our Trade with all parts of the world:

For imposing Taxes on us without our Consent:

For depriving us in many cases, of the benefits of Trial by Jury:

For transporting us beyond Seas to be tried for pretended offences

For abolishing the free System of English Laws in a neighbouring Province, establishing therein an Arbitrary government, and enlarging its Boundaries so as to render it at once an example and fit instrument for introducing the same absolute rule into these Colonies:

For taking away our Charters, abolishing our most valuable Laws, and altering fundamentally the Forms of our Governments:

For suspending our own Legislatures, and declaring themselves invested with power to legislate for us in all cases whatsoever.

He has abdicated Government here, by declaring us out of his Protection and waging War against us.

He has plundered our seas, ravaged our Coasts, burnt our towns, and destroyed the lives of our people.

He is at this time transporting large Armies of foreign Mercenaries to compleat the works of death, desolation and tyranny, already begun with circumstances of Cruelty & perfidy scarcely paralleled in the most barbarous ages, and totally unworthy the Head of a civilized nation.

He has constrained our fellow Citizens taken Captive on the high Seas to bear Arms against their Country, to become the executioners of their friends and Brethren, or to fall themselves by their Hands.

He has excited domestic insurrections amongst us, and has endeavoured to bring on the inhabitants of our frontiers, the merciless Indian Savages, whose known rule of warfare, is an undistinguished destruction of all ages, sexes and conditions.

In every stage of these Oppressions We have Petitioned for Redress in the most humble terms: Our repeated Petitions have been answered only by repeated injury. A Prince whose character is thus marked by every act which may define a Tyrant, is unfit to be the ruler of a free people.

Nor have We been wanting in attentions to our British brethren. We have warned them from time to time of attempts by their legislature to extend an unwarrantable jurisdiction over us. We have reminded them of the circumstances of our emigration and settlement here. We have appealed to their native justice and magnanimity, and we have conjured them by the ties of our common kindred to disavow these usurpations, which, would inevitably interrupt our connections and correspondence. They too have been deaf to the voice of justice and of consanguinity. We must, therefore, acquiesce in the necessity, which denounces our Separation, and hold them, as we hold the rest of mankind, Enemies in War, in Peace Friends.

We, therefore, the Representatives of the united States of America, in General Congress, Assembled, appealing to the Supreme Judge of the world for the rectitude of our intentions, do, in the Name, and by Authority of the good People of these Colonies, solemnly publish and declare, That these United Colonies are, and of Right ought to be Free and Independent States; that they are Absolved from all Allegiance to the British Crown, and that all political connection between them and the State of Great Britain, is and ought to be totally dissolved; and that as Free and Independent States, they have full Power to levy War, conclude Peace, contract Alliances, establish Commerce, and to do all other Acts and Things which Independent States may of right do. And for the support of this Declaration, with a firm reliance on the protection of divine Providence, we mutually pledge to each other our Lives, our Fortunes and our sacred Honor.

John Hancock

Button Gwinnett
Lyman Hall
Geo Walton.

Wm Hooper
Joseph Hewes
John Penn

Edward Rutledge
Thos Heyward Junr.
Thomas Lynch Junr.
Arthur Middleton

Samuel Chase
Wm. Paca
Thos. Stone
Charles Carroll of Carrollton

George Wythe
Richard Henry Lee
Th Jefferson
Benja Harrison
Thos Nelson jr.
Francis Lightfoot Lee
Carter Braxton

Robt Morris
Benjamin Rush
Benja Franklin
John Morton
Geo Clymer
Jas. Smith
Geo. Taylor
James Wilson
Geo. Ross

Caesar Rodney
Geo Read
Tho M:Kean

Wm Floyd
Phil. Livingston
Frans. Lewis
Lewis Morris

Richd Stockton
Jno Witherspoon
Fras. Hopkinson
John Hart
Abra Clark

Josiah Bartlett
Wm Whipple
Saml Adams
John Adams
Robt Treat Paine
Elbridge Gerry
Step Hopkins
William Ellery
Roger Sherman
Sam Huntington
Wm Williams
Oliver Wolcott
Matthew Thornton

1689 the Bostonians followed suit and deposed Andros. Massachusetts and Plymouth were joined together in 1691 as a royal colony.

Pennsylvania was a colony of ethnic contrasts. Its proprietor, William Penn, intended it as a refuge for his fellow Quakers, who were imprisoned by the thousands in England and pilloried, whipped, and executed in Massachusetts as an "accursed and pernicious sect of hereticks." In Pennsylvania toleration was granted to all faiths. Hundreds of thousands of German Mennonites and Moravians flocked to the fertile farm lands of Lancaster, Montgomery, and Bucks counties (the "Pennsylvania Dutch" country). Equally large numbers of Scotch-Irish Presbyterians migrated to the western frontier, diffusing north along the Appalachian slopes to Londonderry in New Hampshire and south to the Savannah River in Georgia. It was not long before antagonism festered between the politically dominant, pacifist Quakers of Philadelphia and the more belligerent, underrepresented frontiersmen of the west.

New York came to the English as a result of three wars with Holland. The Dutch West India Company had founded the colony in 1624, but failed to attract many immigrants because of a policy of fostering an aristocratic clique through the granting of huge estates ("patroonships") and refusing to provide a representative assembly. When British warships arrived in New Amsterdam harbor in 1664, the government under Peter Stuyvesant lacked the support to resist. The English established an assembly in 1683, but its legislation was disallowed in 1685. A rebellion, inspired by the overthrow of James II in England, broke out under the leadership of a German-born trader, Jacob Leisler. It was suppressed and Leisler was hanged, but the independence of the assembly was recovered.

By the middle of the eighteenth century, the British colonies in America—now peopled by slightly more than a million whites and 220,000 blacks—were poised for the move beyond the Allegheny Mountains into the Ohio Valley. But the French impeded their

Above, the Pennsylvania State House, where the Declaration was adopted. Left, the Liberty Bell, which cracked irreparably while being rung—for the last time—on Washington's birthday in 1846. Immediately below, the signing of the Declaration. Bottom, committeemen Thomas Jefferson, Roger Sherman, Benjamin Franklin, Robert Livingston, and John Adams.

Although the Declaration of Independence (left) was dated July 4, 1776, most of the signatures were affixed on August 2. Designed to justify the American Revolution to a "candid world," it was also, according to its author, Thomas Jefferson, intended "to be an expression of the American mind." It proclaimed the doctrine of natural rights and charged King George III with the intent of establishing "an absolute tyranny over these States."

Washington's defeat at the battle of Long Island, on August 27, 1776, forced him to abandon New York City to the British (top left). Immediately above, a romantic rendering of Washington crossing the Delaware in his assault on Trenton, in December of 1776. In the winter of 1777–1778, soldiers at Valley Forge shivered in huts similar to this reconstructed one (left).

progress. Since 1690 a series of Anglo-French wars had spread across the ocean, provoking a monumental contest for control of North America. The French capture of a small expedition of Virginia militia under twenty-two-year-old George Washington in 1754, at Great Meadows in western Pennsylvania, triggered the decisive French and Indian War. It also made Washington America's first youth celebrity. "I heard the bullets whistle," he wrote his half brother John Augustine, "and, believe me, there is something charming in the sound." The letter was printed admiringly on both sides of the Atlantic.

The French had the advantage of a professional army and a centrally governed empire. The British colonists, although outnumbering French settlers fifteen to one, lacked unity. "Join, or Die," Franklin exhorted them in a cartoon in his *Pennsylvania Gazette* on May 9, 1754, but when a month later he presented a plan of union at the Albany Congress it was rejected. Desperate for aid, the colonists requested troops from Britain. At first the British reinforcements suffered a succession of defeats. On July 9, 1755, a British army of 1,459 men was ambushed seven miles below Fort Duquesne (present-day Pittsburgh) and routed in panic, with heavy casualties, including the commanding general, Edward Brad-

Washington bolstered morale with his victory at the battle of Princeton on January 3, 1777. American general Hugh Mercer was killed (near left) in this engagement. On October 19, 1781, British general Charles Cornwallis surrendered his 7,241 troops to the Franco-American army under Washington at Yorktown (above and below). The band played "The World Turned Upside Down" as the British filed by.

dock. Other reverses occurred on the Great Lakes, Lake Champlain, and Lake George.

Then, in 1758, when William Pitt came to power in Parliament, the American arena was assigned priority. Louisbourg and Fort Frontenac, the eastern and western gates of the St. Lawrence, were the first colonial conquests. Quebec fell to the British, although both gifted commanding generals, James Wolfe and the Marquis de Montcalm, were killed in the battle. The capture of Montreal in 1760 signaled the end of the war in America, and the Treaty of Paris, signed in 1763, gave Canada and Florida to Britain (Spain had sided with France) and Louisiana to Spain. The In-

dian allies of the French, however, were not yet ready to surrender. In May 1763, a charismatic Ottawa chief led a combined attack, "Pontiac's Conspiracy," along the entire western frontier that destroyed all but two of the British forts. Not until October 1765, after several defeats by the British, was Pontiac ready to smoke the peace pipe.

Only the distant, shadowy presence of Spain in Louisiana now posed any threat to the security of the colonies or prevented Britain from occupying the entire continent. Yet, paradoxically, in 1763 the government of the prime minister George Grenville de-

31

On April 30, 1789, George Washington, wearing a brown, American-made suit, took the presidential oath (left) at Federal Hall in New York City. He appeared, said an observer, "grave almost to sadness."

Immediately below, Washington arriving in style for his inauguration. Bottom, his public funeral, held in Philadelphia on December 26, 1799. He had been buried earlier at Mount Vernon.

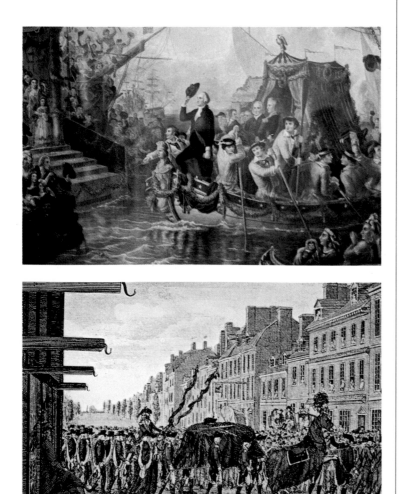

cided to station 10,000 troops in America. In the same year a proclamation prohibited settlement beyond the Allegheny Mountains. A series of measures to raise money for the troops, reversing a century-old Parliamentary financial policy of "salutary neglect," provoked an increasingly strong reaction among the colonists.

The Sugar Act of 1764 imposed a tax of three shillings a gallon on imported molasses. Colonial merchants retaliated with boycotts of British manufactured goods. Spearheading the protest was a rising popular leader in Boston, Samuel Adams, who, said a prominent Tory, could "turn the minds of the great vulgar as well as the small into any course that he might choose." The Stamp Act, in 1765, imposed payments on legal documents and newspapers. In the Virginia House of Burgesses, an impassioned young representative from the back country, Patrick Henry, secured the adoption of a group of resolutions proclaiming the Virginians' right to be taxed only by their own legislature. In the cities, Sons of Liberty organizations forced the resignation of stamp agents and fomented riots. A Stamp Act Congress, convening in New York City, marked the beginning of intercolonial action. "There ought to be no New England men, no New Yorker, and &c., known on the Continent, but all of us Americans," declared Christopher Gadsden of South Carolina.

In England, Benjamin Franklin was called to testify before the House of Commons. "What used to be the pride of the Americans?" he was asked. "To indulge in the fashions and manufactures of Great Britain," he replied. "What is now their pride?" was the next question. "To wear their old clothes over again, till they can make new ones," he rejoined. Nine days later, on February 13, 1766, the Stamp Act was repealed.

Parliament made one more attempt to raise revenues: the Townshend duties of 1767 on lead, paint, glass, paper, and tea. Colonial opposition flared again. The governor of Massachusetts dissolved the assembly for authoring an inflammatory intercolonial circular letter. Once again the merchants adopted nonimportation agreements. The duties were repealed, save for the one on tea. Not, however, before the outbreak of a violent encounter on March 5, 1770, between a stone-throwing Boston mob and a handful of terrorized British soldiers, who on hearing a shout of "Fire!" responded with a volley that killed five and wounded six. Paul Revere, a skilled engraver, circulated his famous cartoon depicting the action as a "massacre"—a coinage that quickly gained universal acceptance.

To this point the Revolution was not inevitable.

Top, Washington with his wife, Martha, and grandchildren in 1796. Immediately above, Mount Vernon. Right center, Washington's bedroom. Bottom right, the drawing room. Near right, Woodlawn Plantation, not far from Mount Vernon.

Above, congressmen and Supreme Court justices meeting in the old chamber of the House of Representatives, in 1822. Below, President John Adams. His conservative policies, particularly his uncompromising stand against the French Revolution, brought him eventual defeat in the presidential election of 1800. He died on July 4, 1826, the fiftieth anniversary of the Declaration of Independence.

Thomas Jefferson (below) held his contributions to independence, religious freedom, and education in higher regard than his accomplishments as president. He died on the same day as did his friend John Adams.

Brilliant, bold Alexander Hamilton (below) believed that strong centralized government was necessary to prevent mob rule and protect private property. As secretary of the treasury, he laid the foundation for the nation's financial stability. His attacks on Aaron Burr, spurred on by his Federalist leanings, led to their 1804 duel, in which Hamilton was killed.

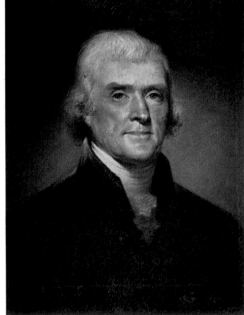

By the late eighteenth century, the press had emerged as a major force in fomenting partisan politics. Below, the Massachusetts Spy *of August 5, 1790. Right, a peace pipe and a medal commemorating Jefferson's treaties with the Indians, who were moved forcibly to reservations beyond the Mississippi River.*

The Tea Act, in 1773, changed everything. In an effort to rescue the British East India Company from bankruptcy the prime minister Lord North obtained from Parliament the repeal of the export tax on tea shipped from England. The import tax paid in the colonies, however, was retained. Further, colonial merchants fumed at the company's plan to market the tea only through company agents. The resentment of the colonists sparked the Boston Tea Party on December 6, 1773, in which the Sons of Liberty, thinly disguised as Mohawk Indians, dumped a shipload of 342 chests of tea overboard. The Puritans, who had outlawed theater, had staged the greatest masquerade in American history.

Parliament reacted to this violation of law and order with the "Coercive Acts," promptly renamed the "Intolerable Acts" in America. The Port of Boston was closed until the tea was paid for; an amended Massachusetts charter banned town meetings and included provisions for a military governor and an appointive council and judiciary; a quartering act required mandatory billeting of soldiers; and royal officers were now tried outside the colony for capital offenses. The Quebec Act, passed at the same time, outraged Protestant colonists by extending civil rights to Canadian Catholics.

In support of Massachusetts, a Continental Congress convened in Philadelphia in September 1774 and adopted a Declaration of Rights, assailing taxation without representation, and formed a "Continental Association" to enforce nonimportation and nonconsumption of British products in all the colonies. Pamphlets were published, notably Thomas Jefferson's *A Summary View of the Rights of British America,* which proclaimed the "dominion theory." Stating that the colonies owed no obedience to Parliament, only an allegiance to the king, to whom the colonists had voluntarily submitted, the document sent ripples through the colonies.

In Massachusetts the assembly, although officially dissolved, began raising a militia force dubbed Minutemen because of their readiness for combat. In response to the crisis the British commander in chief, Thomas Gage, dispatched seven hundred hand-picked troops to seize supplies that were being stored at the little village of Concord, eighteen miles north of Boston. When the British arrived at the neighboring town of Lexington, they found sixty or seventy men assembled on the green. In the confusion a shot rang out, and during the ensuing volley, eight Americans were killed and ten wounded. The American Revolution had begun.

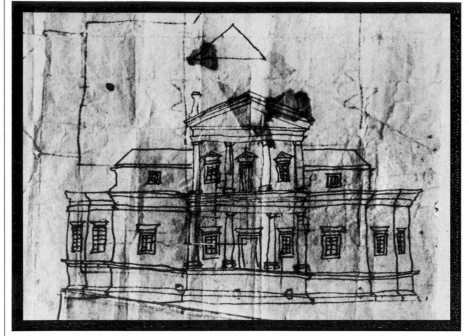

The sage of Monticello

Above, Jefferson's sketch of Monticello, as of 1768. The planning never ceased and construction was never completed. He added the dome, modeled on the Roman temple of Vesta, after his return from France in 1789.

"Mr. Jefferson is the first American," said a French visitor to Monticello in 1782, "who has consulted the fine arts to know how he should shelter himself from the weather." An architect with a perfectionist bent, Jefferson spent a good part of his adult life designing—and redesigning—his Monticello home, right down to the curtains and the parquet floors in the parlor. The conception was more majestic than practical. Unpleasant and unsightly facets of life were hidden from view. The slave quarters were built into the hillside, as were the artisans' shops, supply rooms, and stables.

Further, comfort was often sacrificed to aesthetic considerations. The central eighteen-foot-high parlor, for example, accommodated the dome above more than the functions of daily household life below. The upper level of the house was so compressed that the exterior appeared to be one story; stairways were so narrow that a woman in a hooped skirt could pass through only at great risk to propriety.

Yet the warmth and expansiveness of Jefferson's character are everywhere apparent at Monticello: His books, musical instruments, collection of fossilized bones, and home inventions are reminders of his tireless curiosity and prodigious energy. "Physics or politics or art," commented the same observant Frenchman at Monticello, "for there is nothing of the sort that has escaped Mr. Jefferson."

In 1772, Jefferson brought his bride, Martha Wayles Skelton, to the Honeymoon Cottage beside Monticello, while the main building was being readied for occupation. Left, the cottage drawing room. Right, the Monticello drawing room.

Above, Jefferson at the age of seventy-eight, painted on the north portico of Monticello by Thomas Sully in 1821. Left, the garden façade of Monticello. In this serene hilltop setting, Jefferson lived his last sixteen years, never once regretting his isolation from political life.

Below left, the dining room at Monticello. Jefferson was a generous host, and the expense of entertaining the flood of visitors, who considered a trip to America incomplete without a sojourn at Monticello, impoverished him in his later years. Immediately below, Jefferson's bedroom; the bed was located in an alcove that gave access to the library beyond. Jefferson rose at dawn each day to tackle a voluminous body of correspondence.

The Louisiana Purchase

Robert R. Livingston, the American minister to France, was astonished when, on April 11, 1803, the French foreign minister, Talleyrand, asked him what price the United States would be willing to pay for Louisiana. Nineteen days later, Livingston and special envoy James Monroe signed three treaties granting the Louisiana Territory to the United States for $15 million. The treaties were ratified by the Senate on October 30.

The French bequeathed to the United States 828,000 square miles between the Mississippi River and the Rockies. The richness and diversity of this vast domain were soon revealed by the explorations of Meriwether Lewis and William Clark (1804–1806) and Zebulon M. Pike (1805 and 1806). The acquisition had far-reaching repercussions. It encouraged the loyalty of Westerners who had feared foreign control of Mississippi River navigation. It also saved the nation from dependence on the British navy that would have resulted had Napoleon pursued his dream of empire in the New World. Jefferson's enemies, the Federalists, lost face because they had opposed the purchase. Jefferson's own Democratic Republicans, the country's major political unifying force, learned flexibility when they were forced to modify their strict interpretation of the Constitution to justify ratification. The westward drive to reach the Pacific had begun.

The British continued along the five-mile route to Concord. The forewarned Americans, however, had removed most of the supplies, leaving little for the disappointed British to damage. At the same time, three to four hundred militiamen gathered at the western approach to the North Bridge, across the Concord River. In the exchange of fire, several men on both sides were killed or wounded and the British retreated. During their harrowing return to Boston, concealed roadside riflemen inflicted 273 casualties on the splendidly uniformed British troops.

Boston was now under siege by an impromptu army of militiamen from all over New England. The Continental Congress, realizing the necessity of a formal military force, adopted the Continental Army and chose George Washington as its commander. A formidable presence—"measuring six feet two inches in his stockings"—Washington became the symbol of Patriot determination. Although not an outstanding tactician, he was able to keep a raw civilian army together for eight years. Fearless, ambitious, and self-disciplined, he imbued his motley troops with the spirit that enabled them eventually to triumph despite seemingly insurmountable odds.

The New England troops were put to the test before Washington's arrival. Gage planned to break out

Facing page, top, the Boston State House Square in 1801, the year of Jefferson's inaugural. Above far left, the Louisiana Purchase treaty, with Jefferson's signature. Above left, the threshing and carding of flax in a pioneer village. Far left, a house in the French quarter of New Orleans. This page, top, an archetypical family scene, revealing the new affluence of the American middle class. Immediately above, the dying Indian chieftain Tecumseh, at the battle of the Thames, on October 5, 1812. His death ended a major attempt by the Indians to resist the encroachment of their lands in Indiana and Illinois.

of the siege, but the Americans forestalled him by occupying the Charlestown peninsula, north of Boston, and fortifying Breed's Hill, south of Bunker Hill. The British attacked in three suicidal waves, forcing the Americans to retreat when their powder gave out. The siege, however, remained a stalemate until a Patriot victory, far to the north at Fort Ticonderoga, on Lake Champlain, unexpectedly tipped the scales. On May 10, an expedition jointly led by Ethan Allen and Benedict Arnold overwhelmed the fort's small garrison. When the captured cannons arrived at Boston and were trained on the British, the startled redcoats were forced to depart aboard waiting frigates for Halifax, carrying with them 1,000 Loyalists.

Now the word "independence" began to circulate. Thomas Paine, author of the influential pamphlet *Common Sense*, bluntly labeled George III "the Royal Brute of Britain," charged that there was "something very absurd in supposing a continent to be perpetually governed by an island," and exhorted Americans to "dissolve a connexion which hath already filled our land with blood." For many it was an agonizing choice, one which produced divisions across class lines. The possibilities of open rebellion were fanned, however, when Parliament decreed that all Congressmen were traitors, and Britain began hiring Hessian

mercenaries and inciting slaves and Indians against the colonists. Also compelling was the hope of securing French aid. The decision of the Congress on July 4, 1776, and the Declaration authored by Jefferson were proof to the world of America's determination.

The essence of Britain's failure in the war, despite a superiority of numbers and military equipment, was its inability to subjugate the impossibly long American coastline. The British occupied New York City in 1776, Philadelphia in 1777, and Charlestown in 1780, but the rest of the country remained in the rebels' hands. Two great battles determined the course of the conflict: Saratoga and Yorktown.

In the north, the British aimed to sever New England from the rest of the nation by controlling the Hudson River–Lake Champlain line of communication. After the Americans under Richard Montgomery and Benedict Arnold failed to conquer Quebec in 1775, the British launched a counterinvasion. In 1777, an army under John ("Gentleman Johnny") Burgoyne captured Fort Ticonderoga and continued

southward, expecting to meet a second force advancing northward under William Howe at Albany. Unfortunately for Burgoyne, Howe had gone southward to occupy Philadelphia. At Saratoga, outnumbered, outgeneraled, and short of supplies, Burgoyne surrendered his 5,700 professional soldiers to Horatio Gates' citizen army. This marked the turning point of the Revolution. The chastened British offered America home rule. The French, to block conciliation, signed treaties of alliance and commerce with Benjamin Franklin in Paris on February 6, 1778.

The next two years, nevertheless, were "the times that tried men's souls." At Valley Forge, through the dead of winter, Washington kept watch over the British in Philadelphia with his ill-clothed, ill-fed troops. The British evacuated the city in June 1778, and after an inconclusive battle at Fort Monmouth, New Jersey, returned to New York. In the south, the British under Henry Clinton forced the surrender of an army of 5,400 men led by Benjamin Lincoln at Charleston in May 1780. Three months later, a Brit-

President James Madison (below) tarnished his reputation as Father of the Constitution by his inept leadership during the War of 1812. His critics condemned his nationalistic programs—seemingly a reversal of his early states' rights policies—as a departure from the Jeffersonian principles of personal liberty and a federal government with limited powers. Madison denied the charges, replying that he remained basically true to Jeffersonian confidence in "the capacity of mankind for self-government".

Top left, the British blockade of the American coast in 1812. Bottom left, Queenston Heights, where an aggressive American effort was defeated on October 13, 1812. Top center, Andrew Jackson's victory at the battle of New Orleans, January 8, 1815. Immediately above, the British burning of Washington, D.C.

ish army under Charles Cornwallis routed another American army under Horatio Gates at Camden, South Carolina. Morale was further dampened when Benedict Arnold was exposed as a traitor—he had plotted to surrender to the British the fort at West Point, on the Hudson. The only relief in this bleak picture was the seizure by George Rogers Clark of Kaskaskia, Cahokia, and Vincennes—three key British posts in the Ohio Territory.

With the replacement of Gates in the south by Nathanael Greene, American fortunes improved. Cornwallis allowed himself to be trapped on the Yorktown peninsula in Chesapeake Bay. Cut off at sea by a French fleet under the Comte de Grasse and on land by the allied armies of Washington and the Comte de Rochambeau, he surrendered his army of 7,241 men on October 19, 1781. "Oh God, it is all over! It is all over!" cried Lord North when he received the news in London.

The provisional peace treaty, negotiated in Paris by Franklin, John Jay, John Adams, and Henry

A mangrove swamp (top) was a common sight in Indian-inhabited Florida (above), purchased from Spain in 1819 during the administration of President James Monroe (below left). Monroe's secretary of state, John Quincy Adams (below center), succeeded him to the presidency in 1825. Andrew Jackson (below right) followed as the next chief executive in 1829. Jackson's election was seen as a triumph for the common man.

Laurens and ratified by Congress on April 15, 1783, secured recognition of American independence, the present boundary between Canada and the United States, a western boundary at the Mississippi, and fishing rights off Newfoundland.

Independence might have meant little had it not been followed by the creation of a strong political union, flexible enough to carry the new nation into the twentieth century. At the Revolution's end, the states were loosely connected under the Articles of Confederation, adopted in 1781. The national government had power to wage war, conclude peace, and print and borrow money (so did the states), but not to levy taxes or regulate commerce. The governmental structure consisted of the Continental Congress in which the states were equally represented, with no provision for an executive or judiciary. The inherent weaknesses of the Confederation were underscored by a threatened mutiny of underpaid army officers; futile attempts by Superintendent of Finance Robert Morris to obtain an amendment authorizing a five percent tariff; the refusal of Britain, Spain, and France to grant trade privileges; an uprising of impoverished farmers in Massachusetts under Daniel Shays; and a troubled economy plagued by spiraling inflation.

By 1787 a national consensus for unification had formed. In New York, the Continental Congress adopted the Northwest Ordinance, laying down the policy that the Ohio Territory west of the Allegheny Mountains, after a period of territorial status, would be admitted to the Union on the basis of equality with the existing states. Thus a democratic precedent for national expansion was set. Simultaneously, a convention meeting in Philadelphia drew up a constitution for a vastly strengthened federal government.

Driven by James Madison of Virginia, the framers gave the government power to tax individual citizens and to control commerce. The new legislative body—Congress—was to consist of a House of Representatives, based on population districts, and a Senate, in which each state had an equal number of delegates; a president, with wide powers, would be elected indirectly by an Electoral College for a four-year, renew-

At the Battle of the Alamo (above), on March 6, 1836, all 187 Americans were massacred, including Davy Crockett, holding rifle aloft.

Peg-legged general Antonio Lopez de Santa Anna (above), dictator of Mexico, alternated between liberalism and conservatism. He fought an inconclusive, bloody battle against General Winfield Scott at Molino del Rey (below), on September 8, 1846. Scott captured Mexico City, however, and drove Santa Anna into exile.

Left, the Alamo, a fortified Franciscan mission at San Antonio. Above far right, the first capitol building of Texas at Austin. The refusal of Mexico to accept the Rio Grande (right) as Texas' southern border led to the Mexican War (1846–1848).

able term; and an independent judiciary would be headed by a Supreme Court. Although a bill of rights was not included, it was added four years later in the form of ten amendments.

As a whole, the framers were well-to-do farmers, lawyers, and businessmen, protective of property interests, defensive of southern slave holders, and distrustful of small farmers and city workers. The officials elected and appointed to launch the new government in 1789 reflected these ingrained values. Washington and his vice president, John Adams, were conservative republicans. The elitist secretary of the treasury, Alexander Hamilton, pushed through

the new Congress measures favorable to businessmen: payment of the national debt at face value (a bonanza for speculators); assumption of state Revolutionary War debts; chartering of a Bank of the United States; a mildly protective tariff; and an excise tax on whiskey (which provoked a minor rebellion among farmer-distillers of western Pennsylvania). On the other hand, Washington championed the frontiersmen of the northwest by ordering three campaigns against the Indians. The resulting victories opened the Ohio country to settlement.

The overriding issue that dominated the political scene during the first quarter century of the reconstituted republic was the American reaction to the French Revolution. Washington proclaimed neutrality and insisted on the right to trade with both Britain and France. Each country, however, attacked American commerce, and Britain impressed American seamen and incited the Indians of the northwest.

Rather than allow Britain's provocations to escalate into another war, Washington signed the Jay Treaty in 1794, in which the United States made a humiliating promise not to levy tariffs against Britain. The new nation received in return nothing more than Britain's agreement to vacate western forts it had been occupying in violation of the peace treaty of 1783. American national political parties had their origins in the virulent debates over this controversial treaty. The Federalists, led by Hamilton and hostile to the French Revolution, supported it. The Democratic Republicans, led by Jefferson and sympathetic to the French, opposed it. It was narrowly confirmed in the Senate.

Americans were not the only ones dissatisfied with

The persuaders

Much of America's early advertising was booster talk—an attempt to attract migrants and investors to new communities. Later, business tycoons learned the more sophisticated art of print advertisements, aimed at persuading consumers to buy products they had not known they needed. Mail-order houses were established in Chicago in 1872 with the founding of Montgomery Ward & Company, and chain stores appeared with the Great American Tea Company in 1858. Although advertising stimulated the entire economy, its overemphasis on material values encouraged what economist Thorstein Veblen called "conspicuous consumption."

Skilled promoters learned to attract potential buyers with the associative approach. An advertisement for Coca Cola (left), featuring a prominent late-nineteenth-century opera singer, Lillian Norton Nordica, illustrates the appeal to status values rather than to the qualities of the product. A land sale poster (right), issued after the heyday of the gold rush (which began in 1849), sought to convince settlers of California's farming potential.

Clockwise from left, a 1761 signboard advertisement for a Newport whale oil factory, featuring a whale's tail; a poster for Dr. Pepper's soda beverage, with a mysterious Indian; an advertisement for Green River whiskey, with the standard image of a subservient black; a canister of Sweet Burley tobacco; a container of Sterling tobacco. Tobacco was chewed as well as smoked.

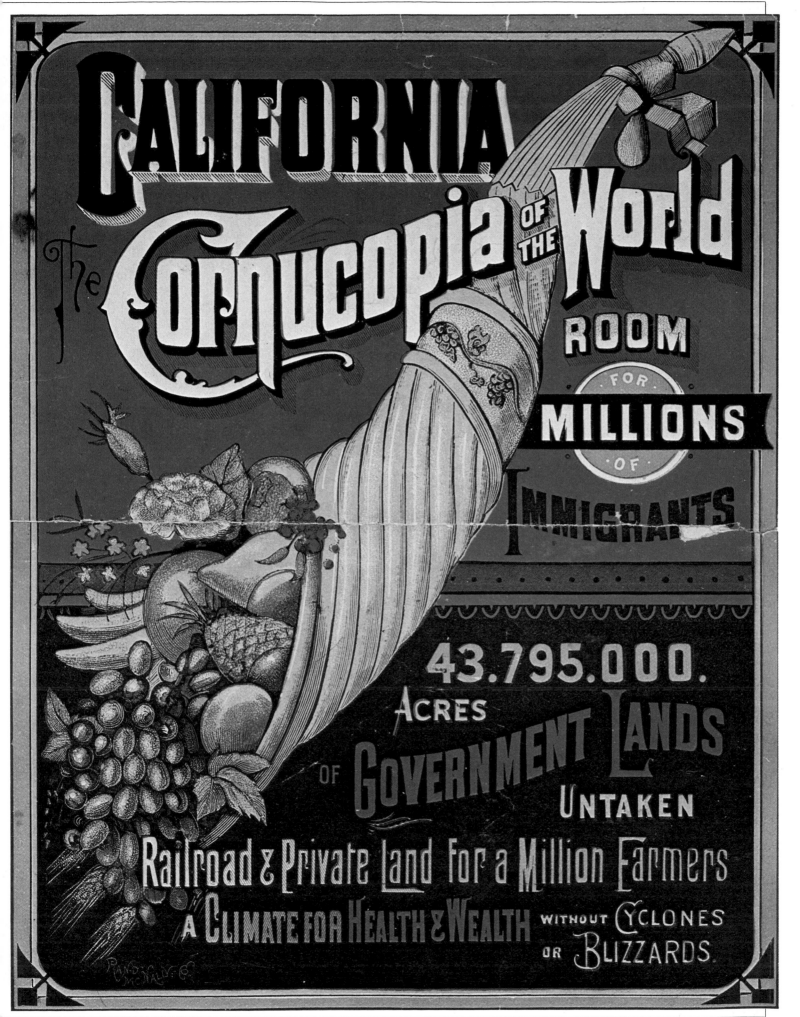

the provisions of the Jay Treaty: The agreement antagonized the French as well. They attacked American shipping and contemptuously attempted to bribe a commission sent by President John Adams in hopes of diffusing tensions. A limited, undeclared war resulted in 1798. The conflict was restricted to naval encounters, but it was disruptive enough to produce deep domestic rancor. The Sedition Act of 1798 sent ten Democratic Republican newspaper editors to jail for expressing opposition to government policies. In answer, Madison and Jefferson authored resolutions adopted, respectively, by the legislatures of Virginia and Kentucky, renouncing the act as unconstitutional. The war ended in 1800 with an agreement by France to terminate the 1778 treaty of alliance and a promise by the United States to drop claims for shipping damages. Adams' courageous decision to limit the war did not save him from defeat by Jefferson in the 1800 presidential election.

Jefferson profited from Adams' rapprochement with France by gaining an opportunity in 1803 to purchase from Napoleon a huge area west of the Mississippi, known as Louisiana, where Napoleon had hoped to develop a New World empire. To this end, Napoleon had shipped an army across the Atlantic. He also hoped to quell a revolt in Santo Domingo led by Toussaint L'Ouverture, "the black Napoleon." France, fearing such disturbances and in need of money, offered Louisiana to the United States for $15,000,000. Jefferson jumped at the bargain, justifying it constitutionally—despite his strict constructionist principles—as a function of the treaty-making power.

The détente with France, conversely, revived enmity with Britain. When a British warship attacked an American naval schooner, the *Chesapeake*, Jefferson obtained from Congress the Embargo Act of 1807, which virtually prohibited all shipping in or out of American ports. Four years later, during the administration of James Madison, the ban on France was lifted but was retained on Britain. Relations with Britain reached a new low when the governor of

Niagara Falls (above left) combines grandeur and utility. The Erie Canal (above), connecting the Hudson River to Lake Erie, promoted westward migration. In the mid-nineteenth century, the gold rush transformed San Francisco (left) from a cluster of adobe huts into a thriving city.

Rebuilding of the Capitol (right, painted in 1835 by Jenneus Bottridge) was begun in 1815 by Benjamin H. Latrobe. The center portion was finished in 1827. The small copper dome was later replaced by a higher, more dramatic iron one, supported on a drum encircled by columns.

CAPITOL, WASHINGTON

The empire city

New York City was the first capital of the young nation, hosting George Washington's inauguration in 1789. By the following year, it had become the country's largest city, with a population of 33,000. By 1860, residential settlements extended north of Forty-second Street, and tracts of pastureland were transformed, seemingly overnight, into city blocks. In succeeding decades, New York emerged as a fulcrum of finance, fashion, and the arts.

A large portion of the population, however, lived in squalid poverty. Disease and crime were widespread, and corrupt political machines ran the government. As early as 1829, a visitor from Philadelphia commented that New York was "more a gratification to visit, than to abide."

New York merchants established regular packet service to Europe and capitalized on their access to the Erie Canal. Immediately above, the ship Leeds *in dock at South Street on the East River, as seen from Maiden Lane in 1828. Wall Street (right), also in southern Manhattan, evolved into a banking center that included the Bank of America, in the foreground with two giant Corinthian pillars, and, beyond it, the Merchant's Bank, also with two columns. In the background is Trinity Church, dedicated in 1846.*

Immediately below, wares being unloaded at the Fulton Street Market, located between South and Front streets, 1828. Built in 1821, the market became a main distribution center for goods that arrived from all parts of the world.

Above, New York as seen across the East River from Brooklyn Heights in 1837. The large white building across the water, left of center, is Holt's Hotel, next to the Fulton Street Market. Casual onlookers (foreground) enjoy the view.

Immediately below, Broadway in 1834, looking north from Canal Street. The English travel writer Frances Trollope in 1831 admired its "handsome shops, neat awnings, excellent trottoirs [sidewalks], and well-dressed pedestrians."

Above, Dead Horse Point, on the Colorado River in Utah, just outside the northernmost boundary of Canyonlands National Park. Below, Bryce Canyon in southern Utah. Its brilliantly hued Pink Cliffs change color with the time of day.

Canada supported Tecumseh, leader of Indian resistance to the American farmer advance. Tecumseh and his followers were narrowly defeated in the Battle of Tippecanoe in 1811 by an American force under William Henry Harrison.

Emboldened by this victory over the Indians, "war hawks" in Congress, led by Henry Clay of Kentucky, demanded conquest of Canada and Florida and security for shipment of western agricultural produce. New England opposed war, preferring to risk capture of its ships rather than cut off all trade. Madison, won over by the hawks, secured from Congress a declaration of war, by close vote, in June 1812. The New England states demanded an end to the southern and western leadership they held responsible for the war. The Federalists of New England never recovered from the charge of disloyalty.

During the first two years of the war, the Americans made several aborted invasions against Canada, two of which led to surrender. The British even briefly captured and burned Washington in August 1814. American naval victories at Lake Erie under Oliver Perry and at Lake Champlain under Thomas Mcdonough, however, prevented a British invasion from the north. The most dramatic episode in the war, Andrew Jackson's victory at New Orleans, was fought without the knowledge that a peace treaty had been signed. The Treaty of Ghent, in December 1814, simply restored the powers to their prewar status. Since Napoleon had already been defeated, the maintenance of "neutral rights" for trade was no longer a serious issue. Boundary disputes and trade privileges were prudently left to be settled when tempers cooled.

A mounted Indian surveys Monument Valley (left) on the Utah-Arizona border. Above, the Grand Tetons, along the Continental Divide in Wyoming. Right, the White River in northwestern Colorado. Below left, eastern Montana plains.

Jackson's victory, scoffed an unrepentant Connecticut Federalist, gave the Republicans an excuse to "brag the country into a belief that it has been a glorious war." The country needed no prompting. A newborn nationalism bloomed. In literature, the tales of Washington Irving and James Fenimore Cooper depicted characters and scenes distinctively American. Even so exotic a figure as Edgar Allan Poe, tormented, he said, by "long intervals of horrible sanity," could not be imagined in any but an American setting.

Industrial self-sufficiency began with the manufacture of textiles in New England and iron products in Pennsylvania, New York, and New Jersey. Eli Whitney propelled industrialization by introducing the mass manufacture of interchangeable parts. The steamboat, railroad, and telegraph revolutionized

The Plains Indian

Spain's introduction of the horse to America in the sixteenth century transformed the sedentary Plains Indian into a nomadic follower of the buffalo—which provided meat, clothing, tepee covers, and fuel. The arrival of the Europeans further disrupted the life of the Indians. Hunting skills soon became martial skills, and tribal youths were taught that it was glorious to die in battle.

Resistance lasted for only a century. Frontiersmen slaughtered the buffalo by the millions. By 1890, disease, whiskey, and army harassment also took their toll. The misguided Dawes Severalty Act of 1887, which distributed parcels of reservation land to individual tribesmen, dealt a fatal blow to Indian life by undermining traditional tribal relationships.

Choctaw Indians (right) play an original version of lacrosse. Below, Chief Black Rock of the Teton Sioux. His horned bonnet crowned with ermine marks him as a war leader. Below right, a Sioux squaw with her children. Cradles such as hers were painstakingly embroidered.

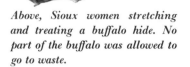

Above, Sioux women stretching and treating a buffalo hide. No part of the buffalo was allowed to go to waste.

The winter hunt (immediately below) provided the Indians with a good opportunity to snare buffalo in snow drifts.

Indian tepees (below left) could be quickly disassembled in the event of a prairie fire, an ever-present danger. Immediately below, an Indian and his bison. Indian hunters exhibited daring feats of horsemanship. Their bows and arrows also proved potent weapons against the whites until the introduction of the repeating rifle in the late 1800s.

Near left, westward migrants with their overloaded wagons. City-bred pioneers often set out with little knowledge of the rigors of travel. Below left, a modern Texas cowboy. Although life on the range was lonely and dangerous, the cowboy adapted well, capturing the nation's imagination with his self-reliance and independence.

communication. Another Whitney invention, the cotton gin, encouraged the cultivation of cotton in the South and gave a new life to slavery. New York City, the entrepôt for cotton sales and the ocean terminus for the Erie Canal, became the nation's premier port. The national population, reported at 3,929,000 in the first census of 1790, grew to 9,638,000 in 1820. Within thirty years of Washington's inaugural, nine states were added to the original thirteen.

With growing self-assurance came less deference for aristocracy. "Did anybody ever see Washington nude?" asked Nathaniel Hawthorne in reply to Parson Mason Weems' cherry tree mythology. The frontiersmen's hero, Andrew Jackson, was elected president in 1828, and his inauguration was heralded as the victory of the common man. Property requirements for voting disappeared, and enfranchised city workingmen began asserting themselves. Jackson declared that "no one man has any more intrinsic right to official station than another," and proceeded to fill the federal rolls with appointees of political machines. Popular politics, however, was not always an improvement. Jackson terminated the charter of the second Bank of the United States (popularly branded "the monster") and helped precipitate a depression. He uprooted the peaceful, literate, farming nation of Cherokee Indians from their Georgia homes, relocating them on strange lands across the Mississippi in Oklahoma. "Such deafness to screams for mercy",charged Ralph Waldo Emerson, was "never heard of in time of peace." Yet only a charismatic president could have succeeded in quelling South Carolina's attempt in 1832 to nullify a tariff law enacted by Congress.

The removal of the Indians was but one phase of the thrust of expansion. In 1810 and in 1813 the Madison administration annexed parts of West Florida in which American emigrants had overthrown Spanish authority; and in 1818, in retaliation for Indian attacks across the Georgia border, Jackson led a punitive expedition into East Florida and deposed the Spanish governor. Spain capitulated, and in 1819 ceded all of Florida to the United States for $5,000,000 and defined the western borders of the Louisiana Purchase. Four years later, President James Monroe,

Top, a mule train heavily guarded against Indians. Immediately above, an ox-drawn pioneer wagon in 1865. Left, a prairie postman. Rural postal delivery put such catalogues as the Sears Roebuck "wish book" within reach of isolated farmers. In these areas, the traveler was lucky to find an inn (below).

The iron horse

The steam locomotive and the iron rail were forces in conquering the North American continent. Although the Tom Thumb broke down during its famous race with a horse-drawn car in 1830, developments of the next thirty years—coal-burning engines, improved brakes, and durable, standardized tracks—made railroads a long-distance reality.

Railroads were initially more expensive than water transportation, but were faster and could traverse mountains and deserts. Seized by railroad zeal, American and foreign investors poured money into private railroad companies, also funded by local, state, and federal subsidies. By 1860 the railroads had received 28,000 acres of land, largely east of the Mississippi.

Far left, top, an early-model twenty-five-ton locomotive. Left center, an 1856 Lake Shore Line poster. The Baltimore and Ohio Line (near left) crossed the Potomac River and the Chesapeake and Ohio Canal. Right, an Erie Railway poster. Below, left to right, a Currier and Ives engraving of an express train; the testing of a trestle bridge in 1869; and Bear River City, a "hell on wheels" temporary town at White Sulphur Creek, Nebraska, for construction workers on the Union Pacific.

The "coming of age" of the railroad era was heralded by the construction of the Union Pacific and the Central Pacific railroads, chartered by Congress in 1862. The Union Pacific was to be built westward from Nebraska, and the Central Pacific eastward from Sacramento, until they were joined. For each mile of track laid, the railroads would receive loans of up to forty-eight thousand dollars and a subsidy of ten square miles of land in alternate sections along the right of way. Since every mile completed yielded that much more profit, the pace was feverish and the quality inferior. Work crews consisting of Civil War veterans and immigrants from Ireland and China were driven mercilessly. The leadership of both companies reaped huge returns by padding government contracts and pocketing the difference. Even congressmen were bribed with shares of stock. However questionable their methods, the early railroad czars managed to join the two railroads within seven years— a triumph that spurred the industrialization of the United States and its emergence as a major power.

Far left, the historic joining of the Union Pacific and Central Pacific at Promontory Point, Utah, on May 10, 1869. Leland Stanford, president of the Central Pacific, drove in the last spike, of gold, after missing with the first swing. Left, an Indian attack on a train. Above, a locomotive at Virginia City, Nevada, during gold rush days.

Cotton was the most important crop in the states of the lower South, reaching into the area beyond the Mississippi River. Above, the loading of bales of cotton on a Georgia plantation.

with the backing of Britain, issued the Monroe Doctrine, warning Spain against attempting to regain its now independent Latin American possessions. America had become free to acquire more territory in the Northern Hemisphere, once owned by Spain but since claimed by Mexico.

In the course of their westward advance, American settlers filtered into Texas. Under Sam Houston, they rebelled against Mexican authority, and, after an initial defeat at the Battle of the Alamo, they victoriously set up the Lone Star Republic in 1836. Pressure for the annexation of Texas to the United States finally resulted in its admittance in 1845 as a slave state, over the opposition of northern antislavery activists. Mexico, however, insisted upon a more northerly boundary than the Rio Grande. Subsequently, President James K. Polk dispatched an American force into the disputed area, inviting a Mexican attack. Polk's ensuing request for a declaration of war, charging that Mexico had "shed American blood upon American soil," brought from

Abraham Lincoln, an antiwar "Conscience" Whig congressman from Illinois, a demand to know the precise legal "spot" of American territory Mexico had violated.

Three American armies quickly overran the weak Mexican forces: those led by General Zachary Taylor at Buena Vista, General Winfield Scott at Vera Cruz, and Colonel Stephen Kearny at Santa Fe and southern California. The Treaty of Guadalupe Hidalgo of February 2, 1848, negotiated by the chief clerk of the State Department, Nicholas P. Trist, ceded to the United States fully one third of Mexico, including the territory of New Mexico and California, for the price of $18,250,000. With the Gadsden Purchase in 1853, at the southwest border, the contiguous boundaries of the United States were now fixed. The acquisition of Oregon from Britain in 1846 had rounded out the empire to the north.

If the 1787 prohibition of slavery in the Northwest Ordinance had applied across the board to all other territories, the domestic tranquility of the Union would have been assured. But each new acquisition became the subject of a fresh dispute, and the country was finally rent in two. In the Louisiana Territory, the issue arose in 1819 with Missouri's application for

Above, a typical cotton plantation mansion. Below, Harriet Tubman (at far left), the "Moses" of her people, here surrounded by slaves she led to freedom.

Above, the painting Calhoun's Slaves. *Senator John C. Calhoun was a spokesman for the slave-holding South. Below left, black song and dance.*

Frederick Douglass (below), a former slave, became an abolitionist editor, a recruiter of blacks for the Union armies, and a diplomat.

statehood. The Missouri Compromise the following year, which admitted Missouri as a slave state, also provided that Maine be separated from Massachusetts and admitted as a free state; the balance between free and slave states was thus preserved. Moreover, the Compromise forbade slavery in the remainder of the Louisiana Territory above 36°30' North Latitude. Jefferson, roused from retirement at his home in Monticello, apprehensively termed it a "fire-bell in the night," and "a reprieve only, not a final sentence."

The gold rush of 1849 induced a coastal population explosion, and with it an application for statehood from California. The Compromise of 1850 admitted California as a free state and allowed the New Mexico territory to render its own decision on the slavery issue. To appease the South, a Fugitive Slave Act was included to combat the "underground railroad," which was helping blacks to freedom.

Neither compromise satisfied Northern abolitionists, who even in the North were often detested but increasingly influential. Among them was a growing number of women, equally dedicated yet denied positions of leadership. In 1848 they held a Women's Rights Convention at Seneca Falls, New York, and demanded legal equality in voting, property holding,

Preceding pages, the Mississippi River steamboat Mayflower. *Top, Abraham Lincoln's childhood home at Knob Creek, near Hodgenville, Kentucky.*

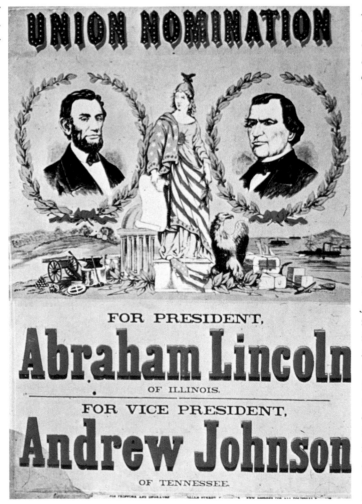

Far left, center, Lincoln and his family on the front porch of their Springfield, Illinois, home during the 1860 presidential campaign. Far left, below, Lincoln's Emancipation Proclamation of January 1, 1863.

Lincoln chose Andrew Johnson (in poster at left), a former Democrat, as his running mate in 1864. Facing page, above left, Jefferson Davis, president of the Confederacy, an overbearing man. Facing page, above right, a Confederate twenty-dollar bill. Confederate troops in Charleston (near right) fired on Fort Sumter across the harbor on April 12, 1861, thus beginning the Civil War.

and educational and vocational opportunities. "But if you ask what offices they may fill, I reply—any," declared the brilliant author Margaret Fuller. "I do not care what case you put; let them be sea captains if they will."

Presidential aspirant Stephen A. Douglas, a senator from Illinois, attempted to solve the slavery issue by proposing that the territories settle the question for themselves ("popular sovereignty"). He embodied this compromise in the Kansas-Nebraska Act of 1854, which precipitated "Bleeding Kansas," armed confrontations at the polls. Roger B. Taney, chief justice of the Supreme Court, offered a judicial solution in the Dred Scott case of 1857. In this landmark decision, Taney ruled that Congress was powerless to abolish slavery anywhere. Therefore Scott, a slave who had been taken from the slave state of Missouri to the free state of Illinois, was not relieved of his shackles because of his new residence. Furthermore, Taney argued, blacks were property, not citizens, and consequently could not sue in federal courts.

Northerners were incensed by Taney's decision, and tensions mounted. In the Senate, a South Carolina congressman, Preston Brooks, beat abolitionist senator Charles Sumner of Massachusetts senseless with his cane. At Harper's Ferry, Virginia, abolition-

Pea Ridge, Arkansas, March 5–8, 1862

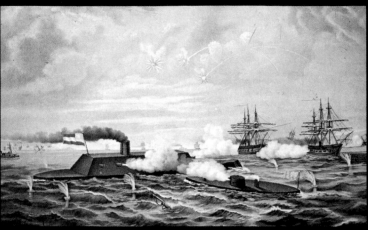

Hampton Roads, Virginia, March 9, 1862

Fredericksburg, Virginia, December 13, 1862

Chancellorsville, Virginia, May 2–4, 1863

Chattanooga, Tennessee, November 23–25, 1863

Lookout Mountain, Tennessee, November 24, 1863

Cedar Creek, Virginia, October 19, 1864

Franklin, Tennessee, November 30, 1864

Shiloh, Mississippi, April 6–7, 1862

Williamsburg, Virginia, May 5, 1862

Gettysburg, Pennsylvania, July 1–3, 1863

Vicksburg, Mississippi, May 22–July 4, 1863

Fort Pillow, Tennessee, April 12, 1864

Kennesaw Mountain, Georgia, June 27, 1864

Nashville, Tennessee, December 15–16, 1864

Five Forks, Virginia, March 31–April 1, 1865

Left, a conference between Lincoln and General George McClellan, sixth from left, after the Union victory at the battle of Antietam, on September 17, 1862. Three years later, Confederate troops evacuated the burning city of Richmond (below).

Union general Philip Sheridan (far right) wrought desolation throughout the lower Shenandoah Valley in 1864.

ist John Brown, hoping to seize munitions to arm a slave insurrection, led a raid on a federal arsenal. His martyrdom in the North infuriated Southerners. Underlying the conflict was the deep-seated Southern fear of the populous North. "Their crime," wrote the Cambridge abolitionist James Russell Lowell, "is the census of 1860."

The election in 1860 of the antislavery Republican Lincoln, labeled "a vulgar mobocrat and Southern hater" by the *Charleston Mercury,* provided South Carolina hotheads with a signal for secession. By February 4, 1861, the six other states of the lower South banded with South Carolina and formed the Confederate States of America. Jefferson Davis, a conscientious but politically inept Mississippi planter, was chosen as its president. Virginia, Ar-

Above, Lincoln conferring with (left to right) General William T. Sherman, General Ulysses S. Grant, and Admiral David D. Porter.

Robert E. Lee (right) signed the surrender to Grant in the McLean farmhouse at Appomattox, Virginia, on April 9, 1865. Grant's terms were lenient: Lee's men were sent home on parole and were allowed to keep their horses and mules for farming. Thousands of Union rations were issued to the starving Confederates. Following pages, Winslow Homer's Prisoners at the Front.

kansas, Tennessee, and North Carolina later joined the Confederacy. On April 12, South Carolina shore batteries in Charleston harbor led by General Pierre G. T. de Beauregard opened fire on federal troops at Fort Sumter, thus beginning the Civil War.

The Confederacy began the war with superior élan, short interior lines of communication, and a cadre of experienced, aggressive West Point officers. The Union had a population of 22,700,000 to the Confederates' 8,700,000 (including 3,500,000 slaves), a vigorous industrial economy, and an efficient railroad supply network—and it had Lincoln, an earthy politician with a statesman's vision.

At the outset of the war, Lincoln denied any intention of interfering with slavery in the South, declaring that the aim of the North was to preserve the Union. Moreover, he was not an advocate of racial equality, although he adhered unwaveringly to his commitment to freedom in the territories. But as the war progressed, Lincoln was pressured to commit the North to abolition. On January 1, 1863, at an opportune moment for the Union, Lincoln issued his Emancipation Proclamation, freeing all slaves in Confederate states. Some 150,000 blacks subsequently enlisted in the Union armies and made a substantial contribution to the federal cause. Lincoln

Gold rush

The discovery of gold in California in 1848 triggered a tidal wave of adventurers who traveled overland along the Oregon Trail or by sea to San Francisco to seek instant wealth. No class or nationality was immune from gold fever, and by 1850, California's population had soared to one hundred thousand.

A series of gold rushes, and of rushes for silver, "the black stuff," followed—in the Comstock Lode in Nevada and the Pike's Peak region of Colorado in 1859, the Snake River valley of Idaho in 1861–1865, the Virginia City and Helena areas of Montana in 1863–1864, and the Black Hills of South Dakota in 1874. A final discovery prompted a stampede to the Alaskan Klondike in 1896.

Few fortunes were made, but the Northwest was settled, and the nation's folklore was enriched by the colorful exploits of Wild Bill Hickok and the rambunctious characters of Mark Twain's *Roughing It.*

Above, an 1871 Currier and Ives print of a California gold mine. The miners in the foreground— at left and center—are feeding a "long tom," or "sluice box." A stream has been channeled through the trough to wash away the dirt and capture the gold on cleats at the lower end. The miner at right twirls a "washing pan" to achieve the same result. The Sacramento River valley (below) was the scene of intensive mining.

Above, a ghost town near an abandoned mine in Nevada. The miners, storekeepers, speculators, faro (card) dealers, and dance hall girls often left as quickly as they had arrived. Many communities remained, however, and helped to populate mountainous regions previously considered unattractive. Left, an Alaskan gold nugget. The largest nugget found in Alaska weighed 182 ounces.

A miner (right) poses with a large nugget in his hand. Such finds were rare, but tall tales of diggers who had struck it rich kept "yonder-siders" from California and "greenhorns" from the East coming in droves. "Pike's Peak or Bust," read the slogan lettered on the side of one westbound wagon, later crossed out and replaced with "Busted, by God."

Below, a group of California gold miners. The common pursuit leveled social distinctions, as college graduates, jailbirds, clergymen, farmers, working-men, and European adventurers labored side by side. They often squatted on government or Indian-owned land.

Left, a California "forty-niner" panning for gold in the Sacramento River. Newcomers, supplied with only a grub stake and a mule, could begin such simple prospecting anywhere. Hard ore, requiring commercial processing, was laboratory tested, as at this lab in Virginia City, Montana (below).

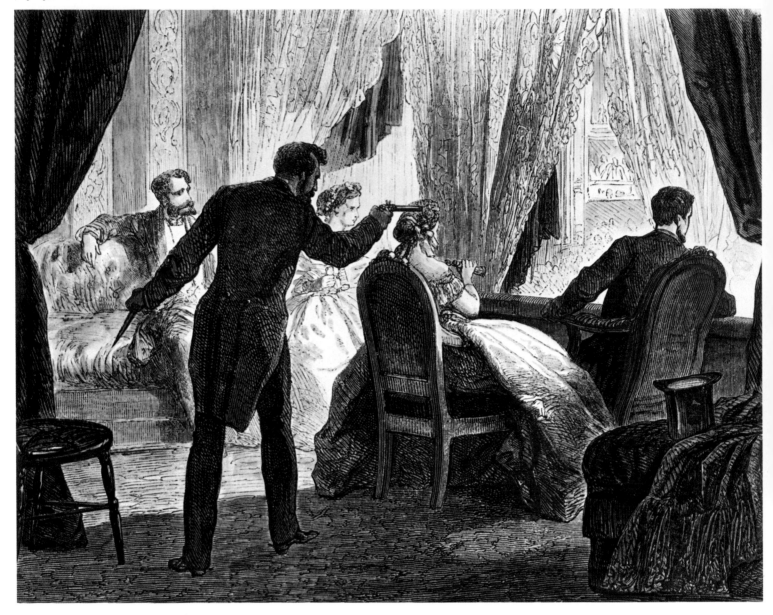

Above, the assassination of President Abraham Lincoln by John Wilkes Booth at Ford's Theater on April 14, 1865. Below, the funeral train that carried his body to Springfield, Illinois, for burial. Had Lincoln lived longer, his humane spirit, magnanimous policies, and political skills might have healed the wounds of the nation he strove to preserve. His successor, Andrew Johnson, was an impulsive man of limited vision who opposed the Radical Republicans' demand for voting rights for the freedmen.

The Sioux boldly resisted confinement on reservations. Above, a war dance. Near right, a rifle owned by Chief Sitting Bull. The Sioux slew all 264 soldiers commanded by George A. Custer on June 25, 1876, at the Little Big Horn River (far right) in Montana. Below right, a Sioux painting of a horse raid.

carried the slavery issue even further when during his 1864 re-election drive he campaigned for the abolition of slavery throughout the United States. The measure—the Thirteenth Amendment—was not ratified until after Lincoln's death.

Lincoln hoped the numerical superiority of the Union would result in an early victory for his side. His strategy—simultaneous drives to seize the Mississippi in the west and Richmond, the Confederate capital, in the east—exploited fully the Union's strength. A string of ineffective generals, however, during the first three years of the war, failed to reach Richmond.

The west was another story; the forces there were commanded by Ulysses S. Grant, an undemonstrative, taciturn West Point graduate from Illinois who had resigned from the service and failed in civilian endeavors but proved to have the nerve and fortitude to win battles. Grant became commander of all the Union armies in March 1864. He assigned William Tecumseh Sherman to cut a swath from Chattanooga to Savannah, with the goal of splitting the Confederacy horizontally and demoralizing the civilian population. Similar devastation was wrought in the Shenandoah Valley by Philip H. Sheridan.

Meanwhile, in Virginia, Grant began his Wilderness Campaign near the Rapidan River. The losses were so staggering that Northern newspapers denounced him as "the Butcher." For nine months, in long trenches, he doggedly laid siege to Petersburg, twenty miles south of Richmond. On April 1, 1865, Robert E. Lee struck Grant's left flank at Five Forks and was repulsed. On April 9, at Appomattox Court House, Lee, in somber gray and wearing a jeweled sword, surrendered to Grant, swordless and dressed in an unbuttoned jacket over a private's blouse.

The combined death toll reached 617,528, the wounded 375,175. The supreme casualty was Lincoln himself, assassinated at Ford's Theater on April 14, 1865. He had projected a permissive reconstruction policy, by which he had hoped to lure the rebel states back into the Union. His successor, Andrew Johnson, a combative Southern Unionist who had been added to the presidential ticket in 1864 to attract "Copperhead" (loyal Democratic) voters, however, opposed integrating the masses of liberated blacks into the Southern governments. The congressional "Radical" Republicans, led in the House by gaunt, red-wigged, club-footed Thaddeus Stevens and in the Senate by volatile, Boston Brahmin Charles Sumner, demanded immediate voting equality (with a consequent Republican majority).

Over Johnson's veto, they passed legislation on March 2, 1867, placing the South under the rule of five military governors who would ensure in each of their districts the adoption of state constitutions, disqualifying many of the former Southern leaders and guaranteeing voting rights for the freedmen and adoption of the Fourteenth Amendment protecting their "life, liberty, or property." A Tenure of Office Act prohibited the president from removing cabinet officers without Senate approval. Subsequently,

Above, Thomas Eakins' 1888 painting of cowboys in the badlands of South Dakota. After the discovery of gold on the Sioux reservation in 1874, a "Dakota Boom" of mining and settlement began.

Below left, a stockade in the South Dakota Black Hills, built in 1874. Below right, Chiefs Geronimo and Natchez of the Apaches. Geronimo was captured in 1886 after more than a decade of resistance.

Johnson was impeached by the House for removing Secretary of War Edwin M. Stanton. Conviction failed in the Senate, however, by only one vote.

Among the "reconstructed" state governments in whose elections blacks participated, only South Carolina's contained a majority of black legislators—and only for a single session. The more usual legislators were white "carpetbaggers" from the North and Southern "scalawags," despised by old-guard Southern whites but often reform-minded. The reconstruction governments introduced public education systems (unintegrated), reformed financial administration, and began rebuilding the destroyed railroad

system. There was considerable corruption, but it was no worse than could be found in the political machines of Simon Cameron in Pennsylvania or Roscoe Conkling in New York.

The North soon wearied of the cause of black equality. The influx of immigrants from southeastern Europe focused the attention of Northerners on issues closer to home. A Northern brand of discrimination—"nativism"—developed in which native-born whites turned against their foreign-born counterparts. Even during Grant's two presidential terms, from 1869 to 1877, when the Radical Republicans were in the national saddle, the Southern whites returned to power

Above, the Badlands National Park in western South Dakota. The badlands are barren and dry, with sparse vegetation, and suitable mainly for sheep raising. The pioneer sod house (right) was common on the plains, where wood was in short supply. It was made of strips of sod turned over in even furrows and cut into three-foot sections; the doors and furniture were made from packing cases. Although warm in winter, cool in summer, and fireproof, the buildings leaked in the rain. Plains settlers built frame dwellings as soon as they could afford them.

Left, Edison in his laboratory at Menlo Park, about 1880. Above, his home, Glenmont, in West Orange, New Jersey. His second wife, Mina, spent long evenings here alone while he toiled through the night in the laboratory. He drew sketches at his desk (immediately below) for the guidance of his large staff. Bottom, a bank of batteries that supplied current for his first lamps.

The inventor-promoter

Although Thomas A. Edison was a self-taught, rule-of-thumb experimenter, his inventions were born out of a sophisticated marketing instinct. In fact, he was an organizing genius who pinpointed specific industrial needs and pooled the efforts of a skilled team of scientists and technicans to satisfy them. He established the first modern research laboratory at Menlo Park, New Jersey, in 1876.

Two of his inventions, the phonograph and the original dictaphone, transformed the home and the office. (The composer Sir Arthur Sullivan shuddered to think that "so much hideous and bad music may be put on record forever.") Edison's most far-reaching contribution, however, was the electric light bulb, which revolutionized life in the cities and spurred urban growth. He also devised the mimeograph, the electric motor and dynamo, the movie camera and projector, and the storage battery. Ironically, he refused to benefit from an equally valuable invention—the hearing aid—though he was hard of hearing.

Edison's incandescent light (left) used a carbon filament in a sealed vacuum. On September 4, 1882, the switch was pulled that lighted forty street lamps in New York City's first electrical district. Top, Edison's gramophone, with a loudspeaker to amplify the sound vibrations of the diaphragm. As a young man, Edison was employed by Western Union, where he patented many improvements of the telegraph (immediately above). Below, an early version of the dictaphone, with a revolving cylinder on which sound vibrations are grooved by a needle attached to a diaphragm in the mouthpiece.

ANDREW CARNEGIE
1. Carnegie Institute, Pittsburg   3. Birthplace of Andrew Carnegie, Dunfermline, Scotland

in most of their governments. Potential black voters were intimidated by terrorist organizations such as the Ku Klux Klan. In the presidential election of 1876, when Democrat Samuel J. Tilden had a popular majority, but Republican Rutherford B. Hayes won a one-vote majority in thc Electoral College, negotiators for Hayes agreed to withdraw the last federal troops from the South and to grant the Democrats post office patronage in exchange for their acceptance of Hayes' victory.

The preservation of the Union assured the continued occupation of the continent. The first transconti-

nental railway, constructed with government subsidies, was completed in 1869 when the Union Pacific and Central Pacific railroads were joined at Promontory Point, Utah. Now the final flood of westward migration began. Clashes with the Indians became more frequent and more virulent. A Sioux annihilation of 264 army cavalrymen led by Colonel George A. Custer at the Little Big Horn River in Montana in 1876 and a federal massacre of hundreds of Sioux at Wounded Knee, South Dakota, in 1890 are only two in a long series of calamitous outbreaks. Wholesale slaughter of the buffalo proved to be the Indians' nemesis. The Sioux under Chief Crazy Horse, the Nez

Left, an elevator for carriages and passengers in Jersey City, New Jersey. Right, the Brooklyn Bridge, completed in 1883, which spanned the East River. Far right, center, an 1885 view of La Salle Street in Chicago, with the Board of Trade Building in the background. Far right, bottom, oil wells in Titusville, Pennsylvania, site of the first American commercial well, drilled in 1859.

Left to right, Cornelius Vander-bilt, railroad magnate; Andrew Carnegie, steel industrialist; William Randolph Hearst, newspaper chain publisher; John Pierpont Morgan, banker, rail-road leader, and financier of the United States Steel Corporation; John Davison Rockefeller, founder of the Standard Oil Corporation; George Eastman, inventor of the photographic roll film and the hand camera, as well as founder of the Eastman Kodak Company.

Percé of Idaho commanded by Chief Joseph, and the southwest Apaches headed by Chief Geronimo all surrendered to the whites.

Before the agricultural development of the plains, a wide corridor from Texas to Canada was used for the "long drive" of cattle from ranches to rail heads, the cattle subsisting on the grass. Then, after the drought and severe winter of 1886–1887, the cattlemen yielded to increasing numbers of "sodbuster" farmers, encouraged by the availability of relatively free land under the Homestead Act of 1862, the introduction of barbed wire for enclosing the range, the wind mill, and the spread of irrigation. Between 1861 and 1890,

signaling the growth that was transforming the West, Kansas, Nevada, Nebraska, Colorado, North and South Dakota, Montana, Washington, Wyoming, and Idaho entered the Union. Utah was admitted in 1896 when it abandoned polygamy.

The expanded railroad network and the broadened use of corporate organization fostered a new industrial revolution. Four entrepreneurs stood out among a rising breed of empire-building corporation heads. Andrew Carnegie, a self-educated immigrant Scot, organized the Carnegie Steel Corporation, profiting from the Bessemer steel process as well as tariffs and railroad rebates to eliminate competition. John D.

The new immigrants

The pattern of immigration to the United States reflects larger patterns of upheaval and change in Europe. The influx of German and British immigrants was decreased drastically by the Industrial Revolution, which provided new domestic opportunities for the economically deprived in those countries. Meanwhile, the fortunes of peasants in southern and eastern Europe took a turn for the worse. The widely publicized need for cheap labor in the United States, the spread of religious persecution, and the lure of inexpensive steamship travel attracted a massive wave of European hopefuls. In the peak year of 1907, over a million uprooted migrants—primarily from Italy, Russia, and Austria-Hungary—left their homelands to seek a better life in the New World.

Top, some of the millions of immigrants who were processed at Ellis Island. After seeing them, H. G. Wells wrote in 1906 that it was the "filling and growing and synthesis, which is America." Many immigrants in New York City worked long hours in sweatshops (immediately above), receiving little pay in return. Left, homeless New York City children in Baxter Street Alley. "There is almost no park or playground for the children," decried public health pioneer Lillian Wald in 1896, "nothing but the sidewalks and streets." Below, left and right, a pair of satirical cartoons in Puck: immigrants being welcomed by Uncle Sam, as published in an 1880 German edition; and, ten years later, themselves scorning the new arrivals.

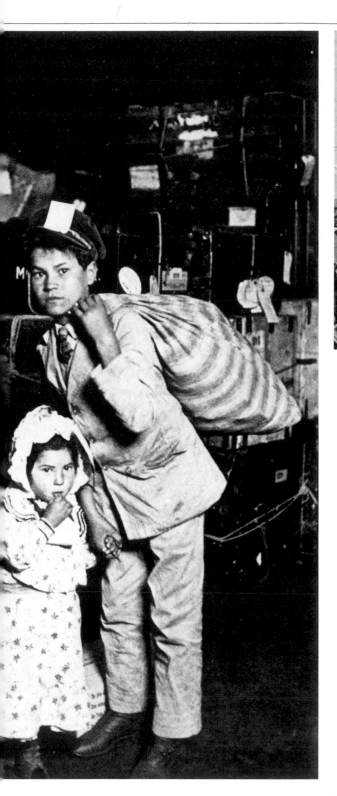

Above, newly arrived immigrants searching for lost baggage. Top right, a detail of S. Waugh's 1885 painting, The Battery. *Right center, a Stieglitz photograph,* The Steerage, *1907. Immigrants who could afford no better had to endure a two-week voyage in these crowded, unsanitary quarters located over noisy engines. As many as two thousand might be shipped in steerage aboard a large liner, providing steamship agents with a thriving business. Right, a line of arrivals waiting to disembark. An immigration official described the reception in 1910: "The immigrant arrives at the Battery. He is immediately and violently besieged on all sides by tricksters and thieves in the persons of porters, hackmen, 'runners' for employment agencies, many of whom speak his language. They profess friendliness and advise him about his lodgings, employment, transportation to his destination."*

Rockefeller, a Cleveland bookkeeper, organized the Standard Oil Company by consolidating distilleries, pipelines, and storage facilities; freezing out competition through railroad rebates and undercost pricing; and eliminating dependence on middlemen bankers. J. P. Morgan, a banker's son, used his control of investment funds to reorganize the national railroad system and to create the United States Steel Corporation. Henry Ford, a Michigan machinist, organized the Ford Motor Company, which, by pioneering the mass production assembly line, turned out 250,000 "Model T" cars in 1914, inaugurating a social as well as an economic revolution.

Apologists for big business, among them the English philosopher Herbert Spencer, justified extremes of wealth and poverty as the social consequences of Darwin's "survival of the fittest," but reformers demanded controls. The farmers' Populist Party protested against deflated crop prices, discriminatory railroad rates, tight bank loan policies, and food processors' monopolies. In response, Congress passed the Interstate Commerce Act of 1887 to regulate railroad rates and the Sherman Antitrust Act of 1890 to outlaw monopolies. Conservative Supreme Court decisions, however, emasculated these measures.

National labor unions attempted with little success

Above left, United States Marines raising the American flag on Cuban territory on June 10, 1898. Many Americans sympathized with the Cubans' desire for independence and saw the Spanish-American conflict as a "splendid little war."

On February 15, 1898, the battleship Maine *(left) was blown up in Havana harbor. Who, or what, sank the ship has never been determined, but the incident aroused violent anti-Spain sentiments, especially in the press. America declared war on April 25, 1898.*

In December of 1898, President William McKinley (left) accepted the cession of the Philippine Islands from Spain for $20 million. Earlier, at the battle of Manila Bay (immediately below) in May, all ten Spanish vessels were destroyed or captured by the American navy. The Filipinos, demanding independence, fought the Americans (bottom left) from 1899 to 1901. Bottom right, a coconut plantation.

to win legalization of collective bargaining, shorter working hours, elimination of child labor, and job security. The most successful union was the American Federation of Labor, led by Samuel Gompers, which limited its membership largely to skilled tradesmen.

Industrialism and the arrival of vast numbers of foreign immigrants bred increased urbanization, and, especially, large cities. Between 1860 and 1900, the proportion of urban dwellers rose to forty percent of the total population. The newcomers crowded the slums of the big cities and strengthened the political machines. These machines, though often corrupt, provided the new Italian, Slavic, or Jewish immi-

A dedicated social reformer, Jane Addams (far left) is probably best known for founding Hull House—one of the first settlement houses in North America—in 1889. Among her other noteworthy achievements was the receipt in 1931 of the Nobel Peace Prize. Near left, Elizabeth Cady Stanton. Together with Lucretia Mott, Stanton led the first women's rights convention, held in Seneca Falls, New York, in 1848.

grants with leniency in the courts, Christmas turkeys, and jobs on public works projects. Reformers were attempting to improve city life by the close of the century, realizing that urbanism was the wave of the future. Free public education; improved sanitation, police, and fire protection services; and settlement house recreation facilities helped. Population congestion and other urban ills, however, remained.

Native American blacks were even more underprivileged: Their most prominent leader, educator Booker T. Washington, urged that they strive for gradual economic independence through vocational education and hard work. Less patiently, William E. B. DuBois demanded immediate equality and pioneered the formation of the National Association for the Advancement of Colored People.

The American presidency grew in power and prestige with the accession of dynamic Theodore Roosevelt (left, bottom row). His bid for a third term was lost to Woodrow Wilson, however, who in turn imparted to the presidency a crusading spirit.

America's emergence as a world power was dramatized by the sixteen-month voyage of the Great White Fleet (right). Primarily intended by Theodore Roosevelt to impress the Japanese with American naval and technological superiority, the venture was, he afterward concluded, "the most important service I rendered to peace."

Women now pressed more strongly for release from legal disability and home drudgery. The National American Woman Suffrage Association was formed in 1890 by Carrie Chapman Catt, Anna Howard Shaw, and Susan B. Anthony, but it needed more than a quarter of a century to achieve its goal. Trade union leaders were also beginning to demand higher wages and improved working conditions for women.

The Progressives—representatives of small-town business reformers, professional men and women, and persons of inherited wealth, some of whom resented their displacement by the arrogant nouveaux riches—threw their energies into successful reform movements. Progressive-minded voters helped elect two Republican Presidents—Theodore Roosevelt and William H. Taft—and one Democrat—Woodrow Wilson—who between 1901 and 1920 instituted law suits against the trusts, strengthened the Interstate Commerce Commission, created the Federal Reserve banking system, introduced conservation programs, lowered the tariff, legalized trade unions, and secured the adoption of constitutional amendments for direct election of senators, the income tax, and women's suffrage.

Once the West was settled, there were "manifest destiny" enthusiasts, such as Admiral Alfred T. Mahan, Theodore Roosevelt, and Congregationalist minister Josiah Strong, who preached that America had a civilizing mission as a world power to spread its way of life across the Pacific. As early as 1867, taking a step toward expansion to the Far East, Secretary of State William H. Seward eagerly seized on Russia's offer to sell Alaska (derided in the press as "Seward's Icebox") for $7,200,000. In that same year, the United States annexed the unoccupied Midway Islands in the Pacific. Naval bases were obtained at Pago Pago in the Samoan Islands and at Pearl Harbor in Hawaii in 1887. In 1890 Congress authorized the building of a major navy.

Yet despite the exhortations of the "destinarians," the majority of the American public remained uncommitted. It was only with the outbreak of the

struggle to liberate Cuba that America's sympathies were stirred. A Cuban revolution erupted in 1895, partly as a result of a depression precipitated by the United States' exclusion of sugar imports. Spanish authorities countered the revolutionists by cordoning off centers of resistance, "reconcentration camps," where many thousands died from disease and starvation. Sensationalist newspapers, especially the "yellow press" of William Randolph Hearst and Joseph Pulitzer in New York, contributed to the public outcries. Some American business investments were at stake in Cuba, but these amounted to only $50,000,000, and other businessmen with concentrated interests opposed intervention.

On February 15, 1898, the battleship *Maine* exploded in Havana harbor. Americans immediately blamed Spain, without waiting to learn the cause (it has never been determined). President William McKinley brushed aside Spanish concessions to American demands and obtained from Congress a declaration of war.

The fighting lasted only ten weeks. Fortunately for the Americans, their hastily and inefficiently organized and equipped army faced Spanish forces even less well-disposed. The Fifth Army Corps of 17,000 men landed without opposition in Cuba in June and quickly defeated much smaller Spanish forces at Las Guasemas, El Caney, and San Juan Hill. Theodore Roosevelt's impulsive but brave performance at San Juan Hill, during which he led his dismounted Rough Riders to victory, helped propel him to the presidency. In July, an American force occupied Puerto Rico with slight opposition.

The war, which was really decided at sea, had far-reaching consequences. One week after the declaration of war, Commodore George Dewey's Asiatic squadron destroyed the antiquated Spanish fleet defending Manila Bay. A second American squadron destroyed a Spanish fleet in Santiago harbor on July 3. Twenty-three days later, Spain sued for peace.

The Treaty of Paris, signed on December 10, 1898, did far more than liberate Cuba. The surprise was that Puerto Rico, which had been granted considerable self-government by Spain, was ceded to the United States; Guam was ceded as well. Moreover, the Philippines, at McKinley's insistence, were given to the United States for $20,000,000. America's Pacific empire by now also included Hawaii, which had been annexed earlier in the year. The Platt Amendment (1901) claimed for the United States the right to intervene in the interests of Cuban security, a move that was abrogated in 1934.

After these acquisitions, America restricted its overseas ambitions to the search for trade outlets. In the Far East, reciprocal trade with Japan was obtained by a treaty in 1894. In China, through "Open Door" notes to the major powers, the United States insisted on equal trading rights. In Latin America, Roosevelt obtained the rights to build the Panama Canal in 1903 by encouraging Panama to revolt against Colombia, its parent state. He also issued a "corollary" to the Monroe Doctrine, asserting the right of the United States to intervene in Latin America as a necessary means of forcibly forestalling European attempts to collect overdue debts.

With the arrival of World War One in 1914, Wilson proclaimed a policy of neutrality, but his sympathies were with Britain and France. The United States was their creditor and a heavy supplier of war materials. In addition there was the emotional tie of a common democratic heritage and the fear of Germany's imperialistic leanings. In January 1917, Germany announced a policy of unrestricted submarine warfare in combat zones and proceeded to sink American ships without rescuing survivors.

When, in March, a revolution in Russia replaced the repressive Czarist regime with the liberal republic of Aleksandr Kerensky, the United States could with consistency enter the war as an ally of democratic powers. In a message arguing that "the world must be made safe for democracy," Wilson convinced Congress that it must declare war against Germany, which it did on April 6. The concerns of America had become global.

The USSR

In October 1902, Leon Trotsky, a twenty-three-year-old fugitive carrying a false passport, stepped off a train in London in the middle of the night and tried to hail a hansom cab. Trotsky spoke no English, and was exhausted after a long, tortuous journey of escape from Siberia. He had become a full-time professional revolutionary at eighteen; at nineteen he had been arrested and locked away in solitary confinement. "My isolation was complete," he wrote afterward. "The vermin were eating me alive. The cell was never aired." The young prisoner had kept his sanity by writing verses of revolutionary doggerel that were, he

himself admitted, "most mediocre"; they later became marching songs of the Red Army.

After several months, Trotsky had been transferred to a small, desolate village above the Arctic Circle in Siberia, where he was relatively free to read, write, and argue with other exiles—as long as he remained in the village. He stayed there four years, until he was able to devise and execute a plan of escape. Leaving a stuffed dummy in his bed one day to deceive the police official who came periodically to check on his presence, he hid himself under a pile of hay in a peasant's cart. In time he made his way to the newly constructed Trans-Siberian Railroad, which carried him back to civilization. He spent the long hours of the train ride reading a Russian translation of the *Iliad.*

Now, on the dark London street, Trotsky, after much vigorous pantomime, made himself understood to a cabman and was driven to 10 Holford Square. There, in a single room with an attached kitchen, lived a Mr. and Mrs. Richter. Mr. Richter's real name was Vladimir Ilyich Ulyanov, though he was better known in revolutionary circles by yet another name—Lenin. It was nearly dawn when Trotsky knocked on the door—"knocking on the door of history" is how one Marxist historian has described it. Lenin's wife, Nadezhda Konstantinovna Krupskaya, answered. The young man excitedly introduced himself, handed her a packet of secret addresses where certain revolutionaries in the Russian underground could be reached, and asked to meet Lenin.

Despite the hour, Lenin, who had been away from Russia for several years, was eager to talk with the visitor, and he pressed him for news from his homeland. By the time the conversation had ended, he was so taken with the younger man's analysis of events that he urged him to remain in London and work with other exiles.

During the day, Lenin showed his visitor around London. "From a bridge, Lenin pointed out Westminster and some other famous buildings," Trotsky wrote later. "I don't remember the exact words he used, but what he conveyed was: 'This is *their* famous Westminster.' The 'their' meant, naturally, not the

Preceding page, the official seal of the Soviet Union, adopted in 1919. The hammer and sickle symbolize the union of industry and agriculture. The inscription, written in sixteen of the languages spoken in the USSR, reads "Workers of the world, unite!" In 1936, when it was suggested that a tractor be added, Stalin replied: "One cannot change the Soviet seal every few years to keep pace with mechanical progress."

Nicholas II (above), a weak-willed and incompetent ruler, abetted the revolutionary movement by his blind insistence on outdated, reactionary policies. Immediately below, a nineteenth-century postcard showing a droshky, or open four-wheeled carriage being driven through the streets of St. Petersburg.

Left, a commemorative poster published in 1913 to mark the tercentenary of Russia's Romanov dynasty. The last czar, Nicholas II, is pictured with his wife and son at the bottom of the poster. Above, a late-nineteenth-century painting of St. Petersburg, the capital of Russia. Below, postcard views of Moscow and the petroleum center of Baku.

English but the enemy . . . the ruling classes. This implication, expressed more by the tone of his voice than by anything else, was always present. . . . To his eyes, the invisible shadow of the ruling classes always overlay the whole of human culture—a shadow that was as real to him as daylight."

Lenin was only thirty-two at this time, but his leadership and decisiveness had already earned him the nickname "the Old Man" among younger acolytes. His physical appearance and personal manner were plain. An American noted that at first glance he "looked more like a provincial grocer than a leader of men." He was short, a bit stocky, bald—just the opposite of the flamboyant Trotsky. Nor was Lenin anything like the orator that Trotsky proved to be. In conversation he was prosaic, dry, unanimated. His chief strengths were his extraordinary self-discipline and his single-mindedness. One of his associates at *Iskra* (The Spark), a revolutionary newspaper, said that Lenin "for twenty-four hours a day is taken up with revolution, has no thoughts but thoughts of revolution, and even in his sleep dreams of nothing but revolution."

Like Trotsky, Lenin had become a revolutionary in his teens—after his eldest brother, Alexander, whom he worshiped, had been executed for plotting to assassinate the czar. In his twenties, he had become a Marxist as well and had been exiled to Siberia. Upon his release, he had chosen not to remain in Russia, where he was sure to be rearrested, but to flee to Europe. Lenin felt that his party—the Russian Social-Democratic Workers' Party, which had been founded at a secret conference in Minsk in 1898—needed a strong, stable organization outside Russia that could oversee and coordinate the activities of clandestine movements within the country.

"We are marching in a compact group along a precipitous and difficult path, clutching each other's hand," Lenin wrote. "We are surrounded on all sides by enemies, and we must always advance under their

The construction of the Trans-Siberian Railroad over 5,787 miles of rugged steppe and tundra was one of czarist Russia's most remarkable achievements. The line, begun in 1891 and completed in 1903, connected Moscow with the Pacific port of Vladivostok (facing page, top). Left, three postcard views of the railroad. Originally the line passed through Manchuria. During the Russo-Japanese War (1904–1905), however, hostile local inhabitants tore up tracks to impede the transport of Russian supplies to the front (facing page, center left and bottom left). After the war, a second, more northerly route—the present one—was built. Facing page, below right, children selling flowers at a station along the railroad.

Владивостокъ

Видъ съ бухты

fire." In this instance, "enemies" referred to those fellow socialists who dared to disagree with Lenin's analysis of the class struggle. Like the founders of the Christian Church, Lenin hated heretics even more than he hated heathens. This became apparent in 1903, when the Social Democrats, after years of arguing among themselves, decided to hold a party congress in Brussels to hammer out a uniform program and an organizational structure.

Nearly sixty delegates attended. Some were from the Russian underground, but many more were émigré leaders living abroad. Although the Russian Social-Democratic Workers' Party purported to be proletarian, it was in fact top-heavy with intellectuals; only four of the representatives were genuine workingmen. To keep their activities secret from the Belgian police, the delegates gathered in a flour warehouse whose exterior was unmarked. (Inside, a large red banner was hung.) Tipped off by czarist police agents and informers, however, the Belgian constabulary knew about the convention weeks in advance. It followed the arriving representatives and harassed them so severely—searching their hotel rooms and baggage, even stealing their briefcases—that they were forced in mid-debate to pack their bags and transfer the proceedings to London.

The debate centered on two questions: How would the party be organized and who would belong to it? Many delegates took what came to be known as the "soft" view, arguing that the party should be as broadly based as possible and should admit all workers and intellectuals who were sympathetic to its general aims. Lenin vehemently opposed this position. He insisted that party membership be limited to those who were able to work for the party full time and that their activities be strictly controlled by the party leadership; the party was thus to consist of a small, dedicated elite. Lenin also proposed to purge the six-member ruling board of the party's newspaper, *Iskra*, so that he would gain control over the board's decisions.

The meeting broke into pandemonium. Friendships of years' standing were shattered. Lenin was accused by Trotsky and others of attempting to impose on the party a dictatorship not of the proletariat but of Lenin. Nevertheless, Lenin, by engaging in tactical infighting, was able to attract a slight majority of the delegates. Lenin's faction of the party thereafter became known as the Bolsheviks ("Majorityites"), while those who favored a larger, more open, and more democratic party came to be called Mensheviks ("Minorityites").

Vladimir Ilyich Lenin (1870–1924) was the Jefferson, Hamilton, and Franklin of the Russian Revolution. In 1900, after several years of exile in Siberia, he escaped to Europe, where he coedited the revolutionary newspaper Iskra (The Spark), *which was smuggled into Russia in false-bottomed suitcases. Below left, the first issue of* Iskra.

In 1903, Lenin was a prominent figure at the London congress of the Russian Social-Democratic Workers' Party (above left). In 1908 he visited the writer Maxim Gorki on the Italian island of Capri (above), playing chess in between arguments about socialist doctrine. Gorki is seen here with his hand on his chin, watching the game. Above right, the street in a Paris suburb where the French Bolshevik headquarters were located. After returning to Russia in 1917, Lenin had to flee to Finland to avoid arrest (far left). Right, a Soviet propaganda painting commemorating Lenin's early years in the revolutionary underground.

In 1904 the czar's expansionist foreign policy led to a disastrous war with Japan. When the Japanese besieged the Russian naval base at Port Arthur in China, Nicholas dispatched Russia's Baltic fleet, under Admiral Zinovi Rozhdestvenski (above), to the Pacific. The ships were bound for Vladivostok, but most of them never arrived; all but four were destroyed in Tsushima Strait (between Japan and Korea) by a Japanese force under Admiral Heihachiro Togo. Right, the battle of Tsushima and Admiral Togo (inset).

Below, Russian sailors and artillerymen.

Lenin's maneuverings led ultimately to the formulation of the doctrine of "democratic centrism," which, despite the opposition of the Mensheviks, was in time to emerge as the cornerstone of the Soviet Communist Party. Under Bolshevism, each level of the party's hierarchy—from the many workers' caucuses at the bottom to the Central Committee at the top—was to be elected by the level just beneath it. This was the "democratic" aspect of the doctrine. Lenin also insisted, however, that the actual decision making was to operate in the opposite manner, from top to bottom: The Central Committee would make all decisions and pass them downward, and all the lower echelons of the party would be bound absolutely by what the Central Committee had ruled.

Trotsky was only one of many who disputed Lenin vociferously on the point of democratic centrism. He complained that Lenin actually appeared to distrust the masses, and he warned of the danger of Lenin's "substitutionism." "Lenin's methods," he wrote, "lead to this: the Party organization at first substitutes itself for the Party as a whole; then the Central Committee substitutes itself for the organization; and finally a single 'dictator' substitutes himself for the Central Committee." (Twenty years later, the rise of Joseph Stalin would make Trotsky's warning appear eerily prophetic.) Lenin, for his part, dismissed Trotsky as a "chatterbox" and berated the Mensheviks in general for their "reptilian vileness."

Although many tried to reconcile the two sides, the split between Bolsheviks and Mensheviks proved permanent. There was a temporary truce in 1905, when, as a result of a disastrous war instigated against the Japanese by the czar, the Russian people revolted against the government quite independently of the Marxists. On January 22 of that year, a Sunday, a peaceful crowd of two hundred thousand unarmed men, women, and children marched through the streets of St. Petersburg to present a petition to the czar. The police opened fire, and about a thousand demonstrators were killed. This senseless massacre, which came to be known as Bloody Sunday, touched off strikes throughout the country. Suddenly, liberals became radicals, and radicals became terrorists. (Lenin, however, like Marx before him, thought terrorism at best a waste of time and at worst counterproductive.) Assassinations, riots, and naval mutinies followed. In the countryside, peasants began burning down manor houses.

Although most Marxists were as surprised by these events as the czar, they moved quickly to take advantage of them. Trotsky re-entered Russia from Finland and set about inciting the workers in St. Petersburg. In October a general strike was called. Banks closed,

Above, an allegorical painting of the Treaty of Portsmouth, signed in New Hampshire, which ended the Russo-Japanese War in 1905.

Disillusioned and starving Russian soldiers (below), on their way home from the front, plunder a canteen along the Trans-Siberian Railroad.

Left, one of the numerous strikes of 1905 provoked by the woeful conditions of the Russian workers. This episode took place north of Moscow and involved more than seventy thousand textile workers. In October a nationwide strike gripped Russia, and workers fought street battles in cities throughout the country. Immediately below, On the Barricades, by Ivan Vladimirov.

1905: "Dress rehearsal" for 1917

The czar's government had hoped that the Russo-Japanese War of 1904–1905 would unify the country behind Nicholas and stave off revolution. Instead, it infuriated the Russian people and emboldened them to press demands for increased political rights. In January 1905, a peaceful crowd attempting to present a petition to the czar in St. Petersburg was fired on by the police. The massacre, known as Bloody Sunday, shocked not only radicals but also the conservative middle class. Factory workers went out on strike, and disaffected peasants in the countryside soon began seizing land. The turmoil ended only when the czar promised the people a Duma, or national parliament.

This demonstration of workers (right) was led by the young Bolshevik Sergei Kirov, who later became a friend of Stalin's and rose to high rank in the Soviet government. In 1934, Kirov's assassination by a terrorist gave Stalin a pretext for a sweeping purge of prominent Communist leaders. Stalin himself may have planned the killing.

Top, The Heroic Presnya. *The Presnya, a large complex of workshops, was the scene of violent pitched battles between workers and czarist troops. Right, czarist soldiers patrolling the district after the revolt had been quelled. Immediately above, government forces attacking workers at a railway junction near Moscow. Similar scenes occurred throughout the country and heightened antigovernment feeling.*

In 1905, mutinous sailors on the battleship Potemkin (above) fired on government forces in Odessa (right). Immediately below, strikers at a St. Petersburg factory.

trains stopped running, newspapers shut down, and economic activity came to a standstill. Along with leaders of the Mensheviks, Trotsky helped organize a St. Petersburg *soviet* (council), whose delegates were elected by striking factory workers. The soviet declared itself to be a legitimate legislative body and began passing laws on its own authority.

After about a month, the soviet's leaders were arrested by the police and Trotsky was exiled once more to Siberia. He never reached the destination intended for him; on the way, he made a daring escape and returned to Europe to write about the lessons of the uprising. He saw in the St. Petersburg soviet a model for future revolutionary governing bodies. Lenin, whose role in these events was minor, later called the 1905 revolution a dress rehearsal for 1917.

On the whole, the years between 1905 and 1917 were bleak ones for revolutionaries in Russia, particularly for the Bolsheviks. Lenin, because of his factionalism, his intolerance of differing opinions, and his invective-ridden, *ad hominem* polemical style, became increasingly isolated from the revolutionary mainstream. Trotsky estimated that in 1910 the party as a whole—Bolsheviks and Mensheviks together—had no more than ten thousand followers in a country of more than a hundred and fifty million. The previous year, Bolshevik membership in Moscow had dropped from five hundred to a hundred and fifty. Money dried up along with support, and to secure funds Lenin began to rely on what were termed "expropriations," that is, bank holdups in Georgia and other provinces of the Russian Empire. One young Georgian Bolshevik who helped mastermind some of the robberies was Joseph Dzhugashvili, who later adopted the name Stalin.

Unlike Lenin, Trotsky, and most other party leaders, who came from educated and moderately affluent families, Stalin had a genuine working-class background. Both of his parents were descended from serfs. As a child, he was often beaten by his father, a drunken shoemaker. Most accounts agree that he was a precocious child, somewhat surly and often humorless. Because he was bright, he was sent to a seminary to be educated. There he read—and the priests confiscated—such "subversive" books as Victor Hugo's novel *Ninety-three*, set at the time of the French Revolution. When Stalin began attending prohibited workers' meetings in a nearby town, the seminary expelled him.

Stalin's activities as a Bolshevik between 1902 and 1913 were undistinguished but perhaps typical for a

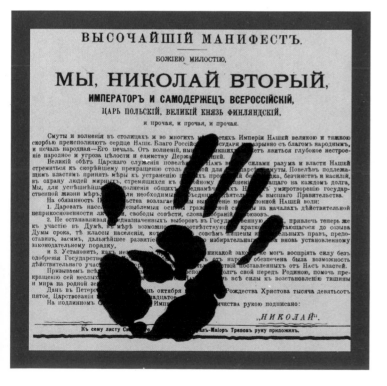

Left, the "Bloody Sunday" massacre (January 22, 1905). Czarist troops killed over a thousand unarmed men, women, and children in St. Petersburg as they marched to present a petition to the czar.

Above, a proclamation issued by Czar Nicholas II that was used as a propaganda poster by leftists, who added the bloody handprint. Right, the first meeting of the Duma (national parliament) in May 1906.

The government's crushing of the revolution of 1905 left enraged dissidents powerless and inspired a stream of hostile posters, prints, and caricatures. Left, a macabre print depicting the Kremlin inundated in a sea of blood. These irreverent caricatures of czarist officials (below) were drawn by Russian artists but published outside the country, in the influential German satirical magazine Simplicissimus. Left to right: Fëdor Dubasov, Nikolai Ignatiev, Pëtr Stolypin, Ivan Goremykin, and Dmitri Trepov.

The frustrations of the Duma (near right), whose powers were increasingly curtailed by the czar, led to raucous parliamentary sessions. Here the delegates protest the repressive policies of a czarist official. In 1906, government forces executed sailors of the Baltic fleet who had mutinied the previous year (facing page, top right). Revolutionaries responded with a terror campaign of their own. Facing page, center right, a revolutionary assassinating a czarist general. Facing page, bottom, a condemned revolutionary scorning the consolation of a priest.

revolutionary. He was arrested eight times, was sent to Siberia seven times, and escaped from Siberia six times. It has been alleged—though never proved—that Stalin earned extra money in these years by serving as an informer for the Okhrana, the czar's secret police. Its agents had infiltrated the Bolsheviks' ranks so thoroughly that even one of Lenin's most trusted subordinates, Roman Malinovsky, was later discovered to have been on the police payroll.

In 1913, Lenin found that he needed a non-Russian party member to present the Leninist view on the divisive question of independence for national minorities within the Russian Empire. Stalin filled the bill perfectly. He was designated the party's theoretician on national minorities and co-opted onto the Central Committee. Nonetheless, he remained an un-

important functionary—Lenin had trouble even remembering Stalin's name. Trotsky considered him a "gray, colorless mediocrity," and his true qualities and character went unrecognized by everyone.

Lenin, although his faith in an ultimate revolution never wavered, began during this period to doubt its imminence. The advent of World War One both buoyed and depressed his hopes. It buoyed them because he believed that revolution was likely to be sparked by the war's mass carnage; it depressed them because many revolutionaries, both German and Russian, became caught up in the fever of patriotism and urged their fellow socialists to take up arms against the soldiers—that is, the workers—of other countries. Lenin (and here Trotsky agreed with him) insisted that the conflict was not a war between

countries but rather a war instigated by the capitalists of all countries at the expense of the workers of all countries.

Before the war ended in 1918, ten million would die and twenty million would be wounded; the Russian army alone would suffer seven million casualties. The conflict practically destroyed the social fabric of Europe. The first country to fall apart—long before the war's end—was Russia.

In March (or February, according to the Julian calendar then in use in Russia) of 1917, food riots and strikes broke out spontaneously in Petrograd. (The German-sounding "St. Petersburg" had been dropped at the beginning of the war.) The disturbances spread. The czar's troops were ordered to open fire on the strikers; they fired on their officers instead

This page, scenes of daily life before World War One (clockwise from above left): a repast in a Moscow tavern; street vendors in St. Petersburg; a striking peasant being forced to plow by czarist troops after the 1905 uprising; and lathe operators in Ekaterinburg, a city in the Urals now known as Sverdlovsk.

and went over to the insurgents. Within a week the czar had abdicated. Prisons were thrown open. Newly released leftists, remembering 1905, formed the Petrograd Soviet of Workers' and Soldiers' Deputies, a representative body elected by factory workers and disaffected soldiers.

Although the Soviet claimed to be a legitimate legislative body, it was in fact only one of two principal nodes of power. The other was the Duma, a parliament—controlled mainly by industrialists and landowners—that had been in existence (though largely powerless) since 1905. The Soviet and the Duma claimed to rule jointly; in practice, however, they

were almost always at odds, each countermanding the decrees of the other. Within a week, the Duma acted to form an executive branch, known as the Provisional Government, to be headed by a liberal Red Cross official, Prince Georgi Lvov. The Provisional Government was to rule the country until a genuinely democratic constituent assembly could be elected later in the year, at which time, it was hoped, a permanent parliamentary government could be formed.

One of the Provisional Government's first acts was to proclaim that Russia would continue the war effort. The Petrograd Soviet thereupon issued General Order Number 1, which instructed soldiers at the front to ignore their commanders and to elect officers from their own ranks; orders from the Soviet were to take precedence over orders from the Provisional Government. Discipline at the front collapsed. The army began to melt away.

The exiled Bolshevik leaders had not expected events to move so quickly. Stalin, who was in Siberia, took advantage of the unexpected amnesty and came

During the 1890s, industrial production more than doubled in Russia. Growth in the steel industry was stimulated by the rapid expansion of railroads. Russia became— briefly—the world's largest oil producer, and coal extraction increased 131 percent. Left, an 1894 painting of a female miner.

From north to south, Russia has three climatic belts: the Arctic, the temperate, and the subtropical. The winters experienced by much of the country became legendary in the West after the Napoleonic campaign of 1812. Above, a depiction of an idyllic Russian winter landscape.

back to Petrograd, where he ran *Pravda* (Truth), the Bolshevik newspaper. Trotsky, who was editing a Russian-language paper in New York City, left immediately for his homeland. Lenin was living with Krupskaya in a cheap room in Zurich. When news of the revolution reached him, he was incredulous. He thought it was a plot by Russia's allies in the world war to replace the czar with a more belligerent ruler.

Once he realized that the information from Russia was true, Lenin spent days on end trying to devise a way to return. It was not an easy task. Between Switzerland and Finland (then a Russian province) lay Germany, which, because of the war, would never let a Russian cross its borders. One plan called for Lenin to disguise himself as a Swedish deaf-mute. Krupskaya told him it would not work: "You'll fall asleep and see Mensheviks in your dreams, and you'll start swearing and shouting 'Scoundrels! Scoundrels!' and give the whole plot away." Finally, the German general staff, realizing that Lenin's presence in Russia could perhaps assist in bringing a halt to the Russian war effort, agreed to let him pass through the Fatherland in a special, extraterritorial "sealed" train ("like a plague bacillus," Winston Churchill later commented). The journey was arranged; after ten years, Lenin was returning home.

The monk, healer, and putative clairvoyant Grigori Rasputin, who exercised great influence on the imperial family, was a ready target for political cartoonists. Above, the czar and czarina in Rasputin's embrace. In another satirical print (right), Rasputin is shown carousing on the top floor of the royal palace; on a lower floor the czar, with the aid of the clergy and an executioner, carries out government policy. Above right, Rasputin—whose reputation as a lecher was well deserved—seated among female admirers. Rasputin's healing power lay mainly in hypnosis, which he used to curb the bleeding of the czar's hemophiliac son.

On the night of April 16, the train arrived at Petrograd's decrepit Finland Station. Lenin and Krupskaya did not know whether they would be thrown into prison or hailed as heroes. As it turned out, they were greeted inside the station by representatives of the Provisional Government, who took Lenin aside and pleaded with him to be moderate and conciliatory during this crucial and delicate stage of Russia's evolution toward democracy. Lenin sullenly heard them out—and then ignored them.

Outside, to a cheering crowd, Lenin said that only the Soviet, not the Provisional Government, represented the will of the people of Russia. He contended

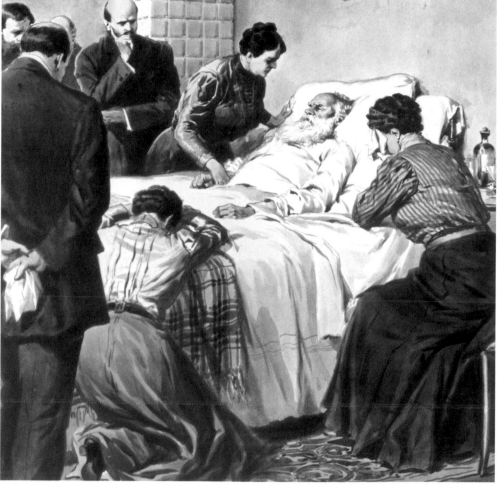

The novelist Lev Tolstoi (above), who scorned the government and revolutionaries alike, played an important role in deepening public contempt for czarism. From his ancestral estate at Yasnaya Polyana (top right), he preached nonviolent resistance to the state. Right, Tolstoi's death in 1910.

that there was no need, as many Bolsheviks and nearly all Mensheviks felt, for Russia to go through a liberal parliamentary stage before establishing a socialist dictatorship of the proletariat—the revolution could bypass that stage. (This was a point that Trotsky, in writing of a "permanent revolution," had been making for years, arguing that in Russia the bourgeoisie would be too weak to keep a hold on any power given it by a revolution and that a genuine socialist, or "permanent," revolution could commence immediately.) Other leftist leaders thought Lenin mad. At the very least, he seemed out of touch with political reality.

The Provisional Government, which enjoyed more support from the governments of Russia's allies than it did at home, proved to be as inept as Lenin had predicted. Eventually headed by an ineffectual non-Marxist socialist, Aleksandr Kerensky, it tried, disastrously, to pursue the war against Germany. In July a brief revolt by leftist workers—afterward disclaimed as "premature" by the Bolsheviks—was put down, and many Bolshevik leaders were jailed. Among those arrested was Trotsky, who had belatedly come to agree with Lenin's concept of a small, elite, and conspiratorial party. Lenin, charged with being a German agent, assumed he would be shot if caught. With

Grand Duke Nicholas (above), the czar's cousin, commanded Russian forces in the first year of World War One. The newly invented machine gun rendered traditional cavalry and infantry tactics suicidal. Below, a Russian adaptation of the British Maxim gun. Far left, a caricature of the czar. Other illustrations on this page depict czarist soldiers.

Stalin acting as barber, he had his familiar beard and mustache shaved off and went into hiding in a cabin in the nearby Finnish woods.

In September 1917, with the Bolshevik fortunes at a low ebb, a right-wing army general, Lavr Kornilov, tried to stage a counterrevolution against the Provisional Government. To suppress the movement, Kerensky was forced to turn to the Soviet for help, and most Bolsheviks were released. At Lenin's insistence, the Bolsheviks continued to agitate among the workers for four objectives: the establishment of peace with Germany, the redistribution of land to the peasants, the transfer of the control of factories from capitalists to committees of workers, and the recognition of all soviets throughout the country (set up on the Petrograd model) as the lawful governing bodies of Russia. "Peace, bread, and land!" and "All power to the soviets!" became popular Bolshevik slogans.

The Russian economy, devastated by three years of war, was in chaos. Food shortages were severe, and systems for transporting and distributing goods broke down. Petrograd verged on anarchy. In November (or October, according to the Julian calendar), Lenin decided the time had come to act. Disguised in a red wig, he returned to Petrograd and confronted a timorous Bolshevik Central Committee. "The government is tottering," he told his hesitant followers. "We must not wait! We may lose everything! History will not forgive delay by revolutionists who could be victorious today."

On the night of November 6, under the direction of Trotsky (the chairman of the Petrograd Soviet), the Bolsheviks seized all the city's railroad stations, its telephone, post, and telegraph offices, the State Bank, and the Winter Palace. (The Winter Palace, the former residence of the czar, was the seat of Kerensky's Provisional Government, which, lacking the support even of its own troops, hurried out of the city at the approach of the Bolsheviks.) With hardly a shot fired, the Bolsheviks had gained control of Petrograd. A proclamation announced that the Provisional Government had been deposed and that power had been transferred to the Revolutionary Committee of the Petrograd Soviet.

The coup was carefully timed to take place just before a meeting of the Bolshevik-dominated All-Russian Congress of Soviets. At the meeting, many Mensheviks and other leftist delegates protested the coup and walked out. As they were leaving the hall, Trotsky shouted: "Your role is played out. Go where you belong from now on—onto the rubbish heap of history."

Lenin addressed the Soviet the following day. To great applause, he announced: "We shall now pro-

The German general staff (above, with Kaiser William II seated in front) spent decades preparing for World War One. When the conflict finally erupted, German armies under Field Marshal Paul von Hindenburg (right) and General August von Mackensen (below) won stunning victories over much larger Russian forces.

ceed to construct the socialist order." The Soviet then began to create a government. The ruling cabinet was to be a Council of People's Commissars. Lenin was to be its chairman, and Trotsky its commissar of foreign affairs. Thirteen other commissars were also chosen—the last to be named was Stalin, who was to be the commissar for nationalities.

Because he had publicly pledged to do so, Lenin decided to permit the long-awaited election of a national constituent assembly. It was a genuinely free election, and the Bolsheviks won only a quarter of the delegates. The assembly met for a day, and then Lenin, his pledge fulfilled, promptly ordered the body

dissolved and sent troops to disperse the delegates.

The most serious immediate threat to the new government was the German army. Trotsky was dispatched to the border town of Brest Litovsk to negotiate a peace with the Germans. The Germans, who were in a position to overrun Petrograd whenever they chose (a fact that later led Lenin to move the new government to Moscow), expected vast concessions in return for an armistice. They were annoyed to hear Trotsky lecture them about an upcoming socialist revolution in their homeland. The talks broke down, and Trotsky returned to Russia to urge a policy of "neither war nor peace," hoping that the Ger-

Early Russian victories in World War One allowed the czar's armies to occupy the Austrian province of Galicia (above). The Masurian Lakes region of northeastern Poland (near right) saw fierce fighting and two decisive Russian defeats in 1914—one dealt by Hindenburg in August and another dealt by *Mackensen a month later (below far right). In November, however, the Russians inflicted some 250,000 casualties on the Austrians at the Galician city of Lvov (above far right). The Germans reconquered Lvov the following year. Below, Czar Nicholas II (seated second from left) visiting the front.*

mans, preoccupied with the war against France, would hesitate to attack. But the Germans launched an offensive, and it became obvious to Lenin that the Russian government had no choice but to capitulate to German demands.

Lenin's view was not a popular one. A majority of the Central Committee, led by a young party theorist named Nikolai Bukharin, feared the domestic political consequences of a national humiliation and fought Lenin tooth and nail. By threatening to resign from the government, Lenin managed to carry his point, but only by a single vote. Meanwhile, the German demands had increased. The Russians were now

to surrender Finland, the Baltic provinces, and the Ukraine—a third of the country's population and more than eighty percent of its coal and iron capacity. After the Allied victory in November 1918, the Russians repudiated the treaty with Germany and regained some land, but the short-term consequences of Brest Litovsk cost the Bolsheviks a great deal of their already dwindling support at home.

The dangerous tenuousness of that support became apparent in the summer of 1918, when civil war broke out in Siberia and southern Russia. In all, three different "White" armies, led by right-wing former czarist generals, mounted attacks against the Bolshe-

Vladimir Ilyich Lenin

Lenin was one of history's most colorless figures. His plain, unaffected dress and manner, his humdrum, matter-of-fact conversation, and his humorlessness and lack of personal warmth made him seem remote even to his closest associates. His capacity for friendship never transcended the bounds of political convenience.

Before the revolution, Lenin's days were spent in libraries, his evenings at political meetings. His home life with his wife and personal secretary, Nadezhda Konstantinovna Krupskaya, was as calm as his political life was stormy. A revolutionary ascetic, Lenin scorned alcohol and gave up smoking as a young man. He loved to listen to music—particularly Beethoven—but feared that it might sap his revolutionary spirit. Another nonpolitical passion was chess, but he eventually renounced the game. "Chess gets hold of you too much and hinders work," he stated.

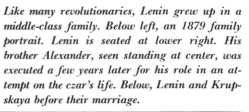

Lenin's correspondence was voluminous. Above, a page of his notes dated February 15, 1920.

The affection that Lenin felt for Krupskaya (above), although certainly genuine, was not demonstrative. After Lenin's death, Krupskaya recalled that on one occasion, during an exhilarating attempt to elude capture by the police, the couple walked arm in arm, "which was a thing we never usually did."

Like many revolutionaries, Lenin grew up in a middle-class family. Below left, an 1879 family portrait. Lenin is seated at lower right. His brother Alexander, seen standing at center, was executed a few years later for his role in an attempt on the czar's life. Below, Lenin and Krupskaya before their marriage.

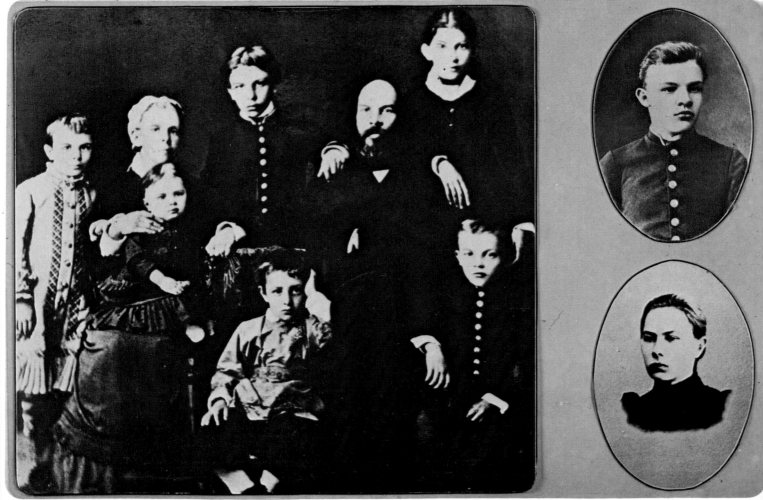

In 1917, in the months before the Bolshevik revolution, Lenin lived in a simply furnished room in Petrograd (above). In August 1917 he fled to Finland to escape arrest and hid in a small hut in Razliv (left). Below, the house in Ulyanovsk, southeast of Moscow, where Lenin was born. Right, Lenin's office in the Kremlin.

Superpowers

viks—or Communists, as they now called themselves. In addition, the Allied governments, largely at Winston Churchill's urging, landed British and American troops at the White Sea port of Archangel and threatened the new government from the north—an act that the Soviets have never forgotten. Both efforts failed. The Allied intervention was too feeble to be effective, and the leaders of the three White armies were too divided among themselves to organize a unified offensive. Furthermore, the Whites' reactionary hostility to land reform cost them the backing of the Russian peasants.

With the regular Russian units in disarray, the Communists in mounting a defense were forced to build up the new Red Army practically from scratch. Trotsky, who was appointed war minister in 1918, was found to be as brilliant a military strategist as he had been an orator and writer. Within two and a half years, he mustered more than five million troops. Former czarist officers were welcomed into the ranks, but their activities were supervised closely by party political commissars to guard against treachery. Traveling from front to front in a special propaganda train to rally the troops, Trotsky succeeded in preventing the disparate White forces from linking up. By 1920 all opposing armies had been routed. Victory belonged to the Reds.

The civil war was a nightmare for the Russian people. Horrible atrocities were committed by both the Whites and the Reds. Thousands of hostages, including women and children, were shot. Most people felt loyalty to neither side—they just wanted to stay alive and were caught in the middle. Worried about its declining support throughout the country and seeing enemies everywhere, the new regime, soon after assuming power, initiated a harsh, repressive policy known as the Red Terror. Opposition newspapers, even leftist ones, were shut down. One of the government's first acts was to create a secret revolutionary

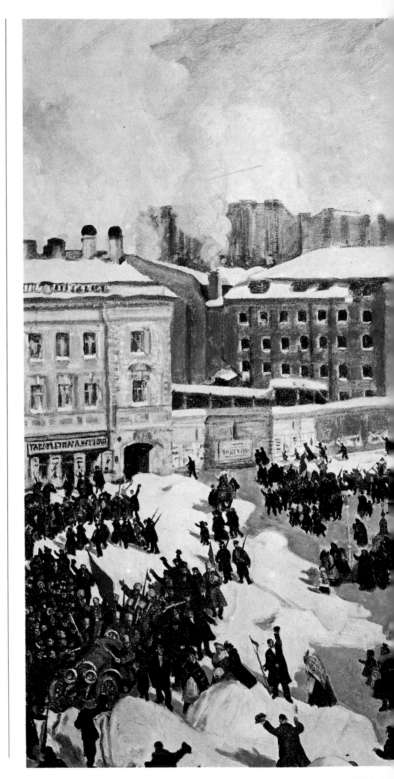

On February 27, 1917, czarist troops in Petrograd refused to open fire on demonstrators and instead went over to their side (left).

Rebellious troops (above) march in Petrograd in February 1917 with a banner inscribed "Liberty, Equality, and Fraternity." Below, two meetings of the Duma. The czar's portrait was removed in the interim between the two meetings.

After the abolition of the monarchy in March 1917, the Duma announced the formation of the Provisional Government, whose ministers (facing page, bottom) were headed by the liberal Prince Georgi Lvov (seated seventh from the left). Angry soldiers (below) burn a portrait of the czar.

In July 1917, disaffection with the Provisional Government among radicals led to a revolt in Petrograd by factory workers and Bolsheviks (near right). When the uprising failed, the demonstrators dispersed (this page, below), and many Bolshevik leaders were arrested.

police force, the Cheka, which was empowered to set up summary tribunals. No evidence of actual anti-government activity was required; a defendant's social class alone was enough to convict him. Grigori Zinoviev, a Communist leader, stated that unlike the bourgeoisie, which confined itself to killing individuals, the Communists would kill whole classes.

Nor were the Cheka's activities limited to the liquidation of what were considered reactionary classes and persons. After a non-Bolshevik leftist named Dora Kaplan shot and wounded Lenin with a pistol in August 1918, all nonparty revolutionaries and intellectuals became fair game. When Angelica Balabanov, a respected revolutionary, protested the execution of a group of Mensheviks, Lenin replied: "Don't you understand that if we do not shoot these few leaders we may be placed in a position where we would need to shoot ten thousand workers?"

The Red Terror was part of a much broader policy that came to be called War Communism. Industry was nationalized, as were banks and all businesses employing more than ten workers. The czarist legal system was replaced by one in which the judges were appointed by local soviets. Trade within the country by individuals was prohibited. Only the government could buy or sell food, which it requisitioned from peasants in the countryside. Anyone who dared open a shop or small factory could be shot as a counter-revolutionary "speculator." Money disappeared, and a system of barter evolved. The government fomented a class war between poorer peasants and more prosperous ones ("kulaks"), whose land acquisitions were resented by other villagers.

In a country that had been devastated by more than five years of war and whose industry was in a shambles—production had fallen by more than eighty percent since 1914—the government's policies were simply unworkable. The peasants, forbidden to sell their produce, began to grow only what they needed to feed themselves. More than forty percent of the crop land that had been under cultivation lay fallow. With almost no food reaching the cities, the inhabitants were forced to flee to the countryside to scavenge; the population of Petrograd dropped by two thirds. Famine claimed the lives of between four and five million people throughout the country.

In 1921 a peasant revolt broke out in the countryside. That same year, at the naval base of Kronstadt,

In the months before the October Revolution of 1917, the Bolsheviks made their headquarters in the Smolny Institute (above right), which had formerly been a private girls' school. From Smolny they coordinated demonstrations against the socialist leader Aleksandr Kerensky (right), who replaced Prince Lvov as head of the Provisional Government in July 1917.

The act of abdication (above) signed by Nicholas II in March 1917 brought the reign of the Romanov dynasty to an end. Right, Nicholas and his wife and children in an official photograph taken in 1915. Three years later they were executed by the Bolsheviks in the city of Ekaterinburg.

outside Petrograd, a garrison of sailors who had been among the staunchest Bolshevik supporters of 1917 mutinied, insisting on participation by non-Communists in the government. The Red Army, under Trotsky, easily stormed the post and destroyed it, but a truly national uprising seemed imminent.

To forestall the revolt, Lenin backtracked. War Communism, along with the "emergency" economic measures that had accompanied it, was declared over. "The greatest danger is to carry the Revolution too far," Lenin said, conceding that Russia was not yet ready for genuine socialism. A program of "state capitalism" was instituted—the New Economic Policy, or NEP—and the right of private trade was returned to the peasant. Although ten percent of the grain the peasant produced still had to be turned over to the government in the form of a tax, any surplus could be sold in the local marketplace for a profit. Heavy industry remained state owned, but light industry was returned to private hands. Shops that had been closed

Lenin was in Switzerland when the disturbances of February 1917 broke out. He crossed Germany in a "sealed" train provided by the German general staff and reached Russia in mid-April. Left, Toward Petrograd, a romanticized propaganda painting that shows Lenin at the controls of the train. Right, another propaganda painting, depicting Lenin among insurgent workers and sailors after his arrival in Petrograd.

Below, prominent Bolsheviks who participated in the October Revolution.

Aleksandr Bogdanov

Feliks Dzerzhinski

Andrei Bubnov

Sergei Kamenev

Moisei Uritski

for years were allowed to resume business in Moscow and Petrograd. The first to reopen, oddly, were the toy shops—their owners had kept inventories hidden safely away in warehouses since the revolution.

Lenin's decision to implement the NEP met with intense opposition within his own party. Many Communists felt that the retreat to capitalism was a betrayal of the revolution's basic principles and complained that the NEP was giving new life to the hated bourgeoisie. Now that peasants were allowed to own land, kulaks were once again accumulating wealth at the expense of poorer peasants, who were not landholders and had to serve as hired hands. Even worse, a new class of small traders and middlemen who bought and sold farm goods began to spring up in the villages. Ultraleftists in the party referred to these individuals scornfully as nepmen and pressed Lenin unsuccessfully to liquidate both them and the kulaks.

The NEP signified an about-face in Communist foreign policy as well. Since the conclusion of the

Yakov Sverdlov

Nikolai Krylenko

Kliment Voroshilov

Grigori Zinoviev

Joseph Stalin

Brest Litovsk peace treaty with Germany, Soviet foreign policy had been bound up inextricably with the fervent Marxist belief that the war-torn countries of western Europe were about to experience socialist revolutions. Indeed, many party leaders felt that no socialist government could survive in a country as backward as Russia unless revolutionary governments emerged in more advanced countries to come to its aid. To help bring these revolutions about, Lenin founded the Communist International, or Comintern. Technically the Comintern was the Third International, successor to the First International, which Marx himself had helped organize in 1864,

and the Second International, established in 1889, which had fallen apart in 1914 on the issue of participation by socialists in the world war. Though the Comintern was composed of socialist leaders from many countries, its headquarters were in Moscow, its president was Lenin's party associate Lev Kamenev, and its activities in all countries were under the strict control of the Russian Communist Party.

The Communists had been so sure of a worldwide proletarian revolution that at first the Soviet government refused on principle to trade with the decadent capitalist governments of the West. For a while, its confidence seemed justified. In the winter of 1918–

1919, revolutionary socialist movements did make advances in Germany and Hungary. These movements were soon crushed, however, and it became clear after a few years that Russia could not count on any immediate help from foreign socialist governments. Lenin announced that Russia had no choice but to cooperate with hostile Western capitalists, at least for the time being. Thus, as part of the NEP, foreign trade with capitalist countries was now recognized as being essential to Soviet growth, and foreign loans were pursued vigorously by the government.

Throughout the civil war and the period of War Communism, the issue of integrating Russia's na-

tional minorities into a coherent federation had been subordinated to more pressing matters. The dimensions of the problem were enormous. In the old czarist empire, which occupied more than a sixth of the earth's land surface, more than a hundred different languages were spoken and fifty distinct nationalities, each with its own customs, dress, and cultural traditions, could be distinguished. Many of these separate peoples, especially the Sunni Moslem tribes in central Asia, had fought the new regime bitterly and had been subdued by force. In 1922 it fell to Stalin, as commissar of nationalities, to put forward the party's decision to grant the larger of these groups nominal

In October 1917, troops loyal to the Bolsheviks (left) converged on the Winter Palace (above), the seat of Kerensky's Provisional Government. Because Bolshevik sailors commanded the guns of the cruiser Aurora (facing page, above left), which was anchored nearby, the Provisional Government had little choice but to flee. Above right, a propaganda painting of the 1930s putting Stalin at Lenin's side during the night of the coup. Right, street fighting on the eve of the revolution. Facing page, above right, a government soldier manning a machine gun overlooking a rebellious crowd.

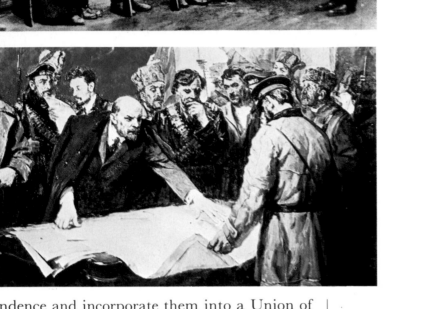

At the Smolny Institute in Petrograd, soldiers stood guard outside (left) while Lenin made plans for carrying the revolution to other cities (below left).

Government resistance to the Bolsheviks was greater in Moscow than in Petrograd, and the fighting lasted six days. Near right, the capture of the Moscow Kremlin.

independence and incorporate them into a Union of Soviet Socialist Republics.

In theory, each autonomous republic would have charge of its own domestic affairs, agricultural policy, and legal and educational systems, while the government in Moscow would control the republic's foreign and economic policies. A Council of Nationalities, with delegates from each republic, would sit in Moscow and constitute one house of a bicameral legislature. The other house was to be a Soviet of the Union, composed of delegates from the general population. Together with the Council of Nationalities, it would choose a Central Executive Committee, which in turn was to appoint the Council of People's Commissars—the actual government.

All this was a façade. Real control of the government lay in the hands of the Communist Party. At the time of the revolution, the party's hierarchy had been relatively simple. Party members elected a party congress, which in turn elected a Central Committee of some twenty members. It soon became apparent that the Central Committee was too unwieldy to handle important decisions, and its tasks were delegated to three smaller organs: the five-man Political Bureau, or Politburo, which consisted of Lenin, Trotsky, Stalin, Kamenev, and Bukharin and handled all general policy-making decisions; the Organi-

zation Bureau, or Orgburo, which assigned party personnel to their various duties in factories, offices, and military units; and the Secretariat, which oversaw the administration of party affairs.

Though few Communists respected him as a theorist or policy maker, Stalin was considered an excellent administrator. The ability of men like Stalin to get things done within the *apparat,* or party machine, was appreciated and at the same time scorned by high party officials, who referred to these petty careerists as *apparatchiks.* Stalin initially served as the liaison between the Politburo and the Orgburo and later, in 1922, became the party's general secretary. As general secretary he was responsible for carrying out the party's day-to-day activities while Lenin, Trotsky, and others pondered more important questions. In time, Stalin came to have great influence in deciding which lower party members would be pro-

Above, Lenin speaking to a crowd in Petrograd from the steps of the Smolny Institute. Left, exuberant Bolshevik troops patrolling the streets of Petrograd in a captured automobile, red flags fixed to their bayonets. Although the new Soviet regime moved the nation's capital to the more easily defended Moscow in 1918, Petrograd was honored as the cradle of the revolution. Upon Lenin's death in 1924, the government renamed the city Leningrad.

moted to the upper ranks; naturally, he tended to choose applicants who would be loyal to him. Moreover, as commissar of nationalities he built up a network of supporters among non-Russian party members. For the most part, Stalin's increasing control over the growing party bureaucracy went unnoticed. Trotsky, who did notice, despised him too much to feel threatened.

Lenin also noticed—and grew alarmed. In December 1922, after suffering a paralyzing stroke, Lenin dictated from his sickbed a last "testament" to guide the party after his death. In it he accurately foresaw the coming conflict between Stalin and Trotsky and gave his thoughts on the merits of each: "Comrade Stalin, having become General Secretary, has concentrated enormous power in his hands, and I am not sure that he always knows how to use that power with sufficient caution. On the other hand, Comrade Trotsky . . . is distinguished not only by his exceptional ability—personally he is, to be sure, the most able man in the present Central Committee—but also by his too far-reaching self-confidence."

During Lenin's final illness, Krupskaya was his main link with the party. Once, after hearing that she had transmitted to Trotsky a personal message dictated by her husband, Stalin telephoned Krupskaya and threatened to have her arrested. When Lenin learned of the incident, he added a postscript to his "testament," urging that the Georgian be removed from his post as general secretary. Shortly afterward, Lenin suffered another stroke and lost the ability to speak. (Krupskaya tried to teach him to say the word "revolution," but the best he could do was "Rev-rev-rev-vo-vo-vo-lu.") After Lenin's death in 1924, the controversial "testament" was suppressed by party officials.

The party that Lenin left behind was deeply divided, both ideologically and personally. The greatest political rift was between the rightists, who supported the NEP, and the ultraleftists, led by Trotsky, who felt that the NEP had given too much power to reactionary elements in the Soviet economy. The ultraleftists believed that the party should insist on the increased collectivization of agriculture and should impose more rigid controls on industry. They sought to spur the production of coal, steel, and other capital goods that would ultimately bring the USSR out of its industrial backwardness.

Trotsky felt that the needs of Soviet workers and those of the peasants were in direct conflict. For industry to grow, he thought, the peasants would necessarily bear the greatest burden. They would have to do without consumer goods, and they would have to

In October 1917, Lenin appeared before the All-Russian Congress of Soviets in Petrograd (above) to proclaim the new government. Below, Lenin's desk in the Moscow Kremlin.

The pre-1917 paintings of Pavel Kuznetsov dealt almost exclusively with Oriental subjects. After the revolution, however, Kuznetsov adapted his style to the prevailing official tastes. Above, a Kuznetsov canvas depicting soldiers and workers outside the Smolny Institute.

In 1917, four out of every five Russians were peasants, and many of them were illiterate. Soon after coming to power, the Soviet government organized volunteers to go into the countryside and teach peasants to read. Lenin (left), accompanied by high officials, reviews the ranks of anti-illiteracy volunteers in May 1919 in Moscow's Red Square.

Appointed war commissar in early 1918, Leon Trotsky (right) immediately set about building up a new Red Army from scratch. During the civil war that followed the Bolshevik takeover, he traveled from front to front in a special military train to direct operations against three separate White armies. He enforced a harsh discipline on the Red Army. Deserters and soldiers who refused to fight were executed.

Above, Red Army troops entering Tsaritsyn (present-day Volgograd) after they recaptured the city from White forces. Left, a Red Cavalry recruiting poster. Right, a Red Army infantry unit of 1920 on parade in the Ukrainian city of Kharkov, which was occupied alternately by the Reds and the Whites. The Whites found their greatest support in the Ukraine.

Leon Trotsky

Any one of Leon Trotsky's brilliant accomplishments—as an orator, a Marxist theoretician, a military leader, a writer, and a historian—would have assured him lasting fame. Transcripts of his speeches, which were often improvised, read like finished literary works. His concept of "permanent revolution" represents a lasting theoretical contribution to Marxism. A dominant force in planning and executing the October Revolution of 1917, he skillfully led the Red Army during the ensuing civil war and thereby saved the new regime from almost certain destruction. For relaxation, Trotsky read and wrote about literature; his *Literature and Revolution* has been praised by literary critics of all persuasions. His frankly partisan three-volume *History of the Russian Revolution,* written after his fall from power, is ranked by some non-Marxists with the works of Edward Gibbon and Edmund Burke for its logic, wit, and style.

As commissar of foreign affairs, Trotsky led the Soviet delegation at the Brest Litovsk peace talks (above), which brought an end to the war with Germany in 1918.

ПОМОГИ

be made to produce surplus food by decree rather than in accordance with the profit motive. Trotsky argued that all wealth in the economy should temporarily be plowed back into industry to provide the much-needed capital required for industrialization, and he urged that workers be organized into military-type "labor battalions" to facilitate the management of a planned economy.

The contrary view was taken by Bukharin, who held no important post in the government but, as editor of *Pravda,* wielded considerable influence. Earnest, sincere, and personally likable—a trait uncommon in Communist leaders—he had been praised by Lenin as the party's ablest theoretician. Bukharin held that the NEP was not only justified but that its "capitalist" features should be extended even further. It might be several decades, he said, before the Soviet economy had advanced far enough to be ready for genuine socialism; meanwhile, the revolution should proceed only "at a snail's pace."

Bukharin also contended that the peasants should not be antagonized by repressive measures but should instead be encouraged to increase production. This could be done by offering price concessions and by making more consumer goods available for the peasants to buy with their earnings. The state would ultimately secure the financing for industrialization by buying up surplus grain and selling it abroad, using the profits to acquire industrial machinery. If anyone was to suffer while industry was being built up, Bukharin reasoned, it should be the urban factory worker, not the farmer. Bukharin's views found much favor both inside and outside the USSR.

Between these extremes, Stalin cleverly staked out a middle position and entered into a troika, or three-man alliance, with two other party members, Kamenev and Zinoviev, to obtain majority control over policy. Few at the time suspected that Stalin would eventually emerge on top; indeed, Kamenev and Zinoviev, who had been extremely close to Lenin since the early days of the party, regarded him as something of an errand boy. It was Zinoviev, head of the Comintern and president of the Petrograd Soviet, who was considered Lenin's likeliest successor.

The troika soon succeeded in isolating Trotsky from power. Stalin belittled Trotsky's contention that

By the early 1920s, years of warfare had caused the national income of Russia to drop by two thirds and industrial production to plummet by some eighty percent. In 1921 a severe drought brought about widespread famine. Left, two government posters appealing for aid to the peasants. The inscription beneath the top one reads "Help them!"

Victims of the 1920s famine (top) numbered in the millions. Communist leaders attempted to blame the more affluent peasants (kulaks), who, according to these two propaganda drawings (above), demonstrated their resistance to socialism by withholding grain from the poorer peasants. Right, a poster by the Czech artist Alphonse Mucha, inspired by the disastrous conditions in Soviet Russia.

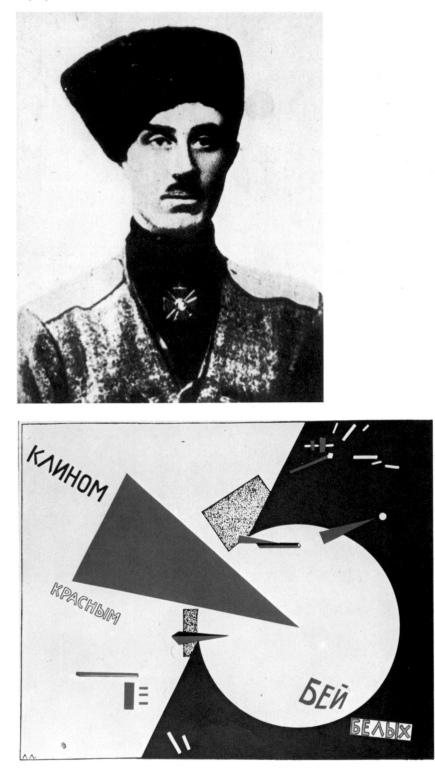

it was necessary to foment revolutions abroad to come to the Soviet Union's aid, insisting that, despite Marx, it would be possible to build "socialism in one country." Trotsky's brief siding with the Mensheviks in 1903 and his disputes with Lenin right up until 1917 were played up in the party press. Zinoviev even urged that Trotsky be arrested, but Stalin restrained him, saying that Trotsky was still too popular with the people. Kamenev and Zinoviev openly snubbed Trotsky at Politburo meetings; Stalin, however, continued to greet him warmly in public.

Even Trotsky's admirers admit that he put up a poor fight. He had been ill with a mysterious fever at

After the Bolshevik coup d'état, Baron Pëtr Wrangel (top left) led a White army against the Soviets. In November 1920 he was soundly defeated by the Red Army and fled with some 130,000 of his troops to Turkey. The collapse of Wrangel's army signaled the end of organized White resistance. Above left, Beat the Whites with the Red Wedge, *a poster by El Lissitzky, a noted exponent of the Constructivist school in the USSR.*

Political commissars were appointed to watch over Red Army officers at the front. Above, a painting of the death of a commissar. Facing page, above right, a caricature of an official of the anti-Bolshevik Ukrainian government. Facing page, below right, a Polish postcard marking Poland's liberation from Germany and Russia. Following pages, a huge parade in Moscow's Red Square celebrating the Bolshevik triumph in Russia.

the time of Lenin's death, and had fallen into a prolonged state of lassitude during the crucial months afterward. Moreover, his pride and his absolute conviction that his views would ultimately prevail made him unsuited for squalid party infighting. Trotsky continued to lead a "Left Opposition" against the troika, complaining about the rising power of the bureaucracy and the absence of "free discussion" within the party. In 1925, Stalin managed to engineer Trotsky's dismissal as war commissar. Obedient to the party's will, Trotsky surrendered control of his greatest source of power, the Red Army.

Once it became clear that Trotsky's political for-tunes were on the decline, Stalin decided to join forces with Bukharin to discredit Kamenev and Zinoviev. The latter two, thoroughly frightened by Stalin's plotting and lack of political scruples, met secretly with Trotsky in 1926 and formed the Joint Opposition. The alliance was short-lived. Party underlings, completely subservient to Stalin, passed a measure prohibiting "factionalism," and Kamenev and Zinoviev were expelled from the party. (Later, after both agreed to repudiate "Trotskyism," they were readmitted but were allowed to play only subordinate roles.) Trotsky was ousted from the Politburo in 1926 and from the party in 1927, exiled to

In medieval Russia, every major city had a kremlin, or central fortress, containing governmental offices, palaces for princes and bishops, marketplaces, armories, and cathedrals. Above, the seventeenth-century Church of the Nativity in the Moscow Kremlin.

The modern Palace of the Supreme Soviet (above) was built after the revolution to house the USSR's highest legislative body. Right, the fifteenth-century Cathedral of the Annunciation.

St. Basil's Cathedral (left), begun by Czar Ivan the Terrible in 1554, is surmounted by a dozen multicolored domes and spires. The Kremlin's architecture reflects Byzantine, Russian Baroque, and Italian Renaissance influence. Immediately below, the czar's bedroom in the Belvedere Palace. This page, bottom left, a small enclosure for religious relics in the Cathedral of the Assumption. This page, bottom right, the throne room in the Granovitaya Palace.

The Kremlin

In March 1918, fearful that Petrograd might be captured by hostile German or Allied forces, Lenin and Trotsky persuaded a reluctant Central Committee to move the capital of Russia to the relative safety of Moscow. They took up quarters in the Kremlin, a ninety-acre triangular-shaped walled fortress that had been the seat of the Russian Orthodox Church since 1326 and the seat of government until 1712, when Peter the Great moved the capital to St. Petersburg.

Trotsky did not like his new quarters. "Everything in the room was incompatible with work. The aroma of the idle life of the master class emanated from every chair." A clock decorated with a carved Cupid and Psyche especially annoyed him. He wrote of his first day in Moscow, when he and Lenin were in conference: "Cupid and his Psyche interrupted us with their singing, silver bells. We looked at each other as if we had both caught ourselves thinking the same thing; we were being overheard by the past, lurking over there in the corner.... We treated it without respect, but without hostility, either; rather, with a touch of irony."

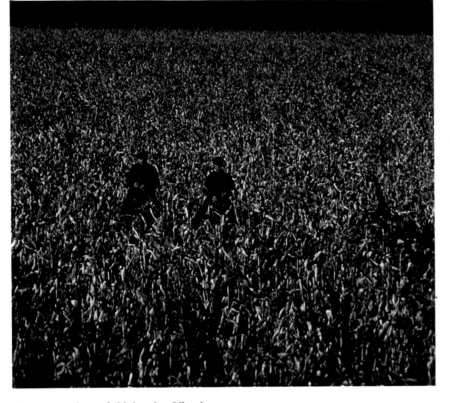

Above, a wheat field in the Ukraine. When the Soviet government created **kolkhozes** *(collective farms), peasants were granted deeds of concession (below), that allowed them to keep small garden plots for their own use.*

Turkestan in 1928, and banished to Turkey in 1929.

Having disposed of his more serious rivals, Stalin now rid himself of Bukharin by having him removed from the Politburo. He also discarded Bukharin's gradualist policies and began to push through the very programs for which he had castigated Trotsky a few years before. The result, in 1928, was the proclamation of the First Five-Year Plan. All industry was nationalized and put under the control of the State Planning Commission, or Gosplan, which set impossibly ambitious production goals. Gosplan's engineers and statisticians allocated all raw materials, set priorities for the use of rail facilities, and resettled hun-

dreds of thousands of workers in targeted areas. Consumer goods invariably received a low priority; the emphasis was on steel, coal, and electrical power. Factory managers who did not meet extremely high quotas were declared "wreckers" and punished.

Other Five-Year Plans followed, and every medium of government propaganda was directed toward romanticizing the heroic worker. Individuals were given explicit quotas and urged to exceed them. Some did so. During one hectic six-hour shift in 1935, a young miner named Alexei Stakhanov, by improving the efficiency of work procedures, managed to dig 102 tons of coal—some fifteen times the average. He

Center, reapers on a kolkhoz in the Ukraine. Left, a 1931 poster exhorting kolkhoz farmers to sow according to the "Bolshevik plan." Sunflowers (above) and corn (below) are cultivated extensively in the Ukraine.

was immediately hailed as a national hero, and a new movement, Stakhanovism, was inaugurated by the government to inspire workers in other industries to break production records. Workers who distinguished themselves as Stakhanovites were rewarded with higher pay, better living quarters, and paid vacations at state resorts. The lot of ordinary workers was grimmer: long hours, low pay, and almost no chance of changing jobs.

Because consumer goods were de-emphasized, the Five-Year Plans did little to improve the quality of life of the Soviet people. Industrial production, however, rose significantly. During the 1930s, the gross national product of the Soviet Union increased by fifteen to eighteen percent a year, whereas that of the Depression-ridden United States actually declined.

Stalin also co-opted Trotsky's views on the collectivization of agriculture, but he carried out these policies with a harshness and a vengeance that appalled his former rival. First he confiscated the grain and livestock of the kulaks. Then he ordered the peasants to join *kolkhozes,* or collectives. The kolkhoz was to own most of the land and livestock, individual peasants being permitted only a small garden plot and perhaps a few farm animals. Though the kolkhoz was in theory owned by the peasants who belonged to it,

Electrification

By the early 1920s, after several years of "War Communism," severe famine, and economic chaos, it became apparent to Lenin and others that the USSR was not yet ready for genuine socialism. Lenin proposed, as an interim measure, the New Economic Policy (NEP), which would restore some degree of free trade to the peasants and permit private businesses to reopen in the cities. Under the NEP, centralized planning of the economy as a whole was to be de-emphasized in favor of laissez faire.

Lenin decided, however, that it was absolutely essential, if only for psychological reasons, to retain and even intensify government control over certain segments of the economy—particularly electrification. "To work!" he told the Soviet people, "and in ten to twenty years' time all Russia—industrial and agricultural—will be electrified!" In 1920 the government appointed a special commission for national electrification, a body expanded a year later into the State Planning Commission (Gosplan). The commission's task was formidable: It was reported that for several years the door on the Gosplan building bore the notice "Please knock. The electric bell does not work."

Lenin's obsession with electrification as the focus for centralized government control of the economy led to the hasty formulation of a nationwide plan for building dams and power stations. "It must be announced at once," he said, "in a graphic, popular form, in order to captivate the masses by a clear and brilliant prospect." Above, a propaganda poster bearing Lenin's famous slogan "Communism equals Soviet power plus electrification."

Below, a painting of a hydroelectric dam under construction in the Caucasus.

In photographs and posters, government propagandists tried to transform the public's enthusiasm for electrification into an enthusiasm for Communism as well. The photogenic qualities of the massive turbines found in generating stations (left) made the turbines powerful symbols of technological progress in the Soviet state. Below, four panels by the poet and artist Vladimir Mayakovski for a poster attributing the benefits of electrification to the foresight of the Soviet government.

When electricity was brought to Uzbekistan, the nomadic peoples of the region (left) greeted it with a mixture of bewilderment and awe. Light bulbs were called Ilyich's lamps, in honor of Lenin.

Right, a power line in the Kirghiz SSR, a mountainous Soviet republic that borders on China in central Asia.

the production quotas were set in Moscow, and its produce was turned over to the government. All equipment on the kolkhoz was rented from regional government-controlled machine-tractor stations, which also served as collection agencies for the produce and kept an eye on the everyday operations of the kolkhoz.

Collectives, however, were to be but an intermediate step. The ultimate goal was to put all farm workers on *sovkhozes,* or large state farms, which were operated more like factories than farms. Peasants worked on sovkhozes for daily wages, with no rights to individual garden plots or control over surpluses.

The sovkhoz remains to this day the ideal Soviet farm complex. Each sovkhoz is specialized—grain, meat, poultry, or dairy products, for example—and has its own dormitories, kitchens, communal dining rooms, and repair shops, along with an agricultural school. The main political purpose of the sovkhoz was to eliminate class conflicts by transforming the rural peasant into something resembling an urban proletarian factory worker.

Simply describing a kolkhoz or a sovkhoz gives no idea of the wrenching horror that convulsed the Soviet countryside when Stalin's measures were abruptly and brutally put into effect. Approximately

During the years of "War Communism" immediately following the revolution, a period in which all private business was expropriated, inflation rendered Russian currency virtually worthless. Left, a thousand-rouble banknote issued in 1919. Within a few years, it was worth no more than a single American penny.

In 1924 the government introduced a currency reform to stop inflation. Above, a poster reading in part: "Bourgeois, say goodbye to the days of plenty." The panels on the left depict the economic chaos that prevailed in the period preceding the reform; those on the right show the benefits brought by the new currency.

two million kulaks, along with their families, were either machine-gunned by party execution squads or deported to labor camps. On learning that their meager plots were about to be expropriated, peasants burned their crops in fury and butchered and ate their animals rather than surrender them to the government. Two thirds of all the sheep and goats in the USSR, forty-five percent of the cattle, and more than half the horses were slaughtered by their owners within a few months.

The peasants' will was broken in the winter of 1932–1933 by a government measure that seemed almost unthinkable. The state, after gathering up all the grain from the harvest of 1932, withheld it from the countryside. The result was a deliberately created famine of awful proportions—one of the worst in human history. Eyewitness reports told of whole villages deserted, roaming bands of starving peasants, and incidents of cannibalism. Some have calculated that at least ten million peasants died during this period. Between four and five million starved to death in the Ukraine alone.

Idealistic supporters of the revolution were horrified. Like many writers, the poet and novelist Boris Pasternak visited the countryside with the aim of gathering material for an optimistic book about col-

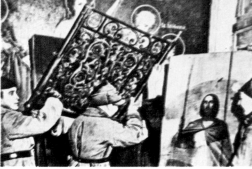

Soviet leaders used the country's economic woes as a pretext for confiscating the wealth of the Church (above) and "returning it to the people." Right, a poster celebrating the seventh anniversary of the revolution. Below, a poster from the Soviet government's antiprostitution campaign.

Poet of the revolution

As a schoolboy, Vladimir Mayakovski (1893–1930) embraced revolutionary politics wholeheartedly and was arrested three times for underground activities. He began writing poetry at sixteen, while in solitary confinement. Upon his release from prison in 1910 he attended Moscow Art School and became a prominent spokesman for Futurism, a defiantly modernistic movement that glorified the machine age. In his poetry, Mayakovski sought to "depoetize" traditional verse conventions by using crude slang, distorted rhythms and assonances, dazzling verbal innovations, and a bold, staccato diction that readily lent itself to declamation.

After 1917, Mayakovski emerged as the Soviet regime's chief poet, graphic artist, and propagandist. Ironically, his conviction that a revolutionary society required new forms of artistic expression brought him into direct conflict with the regime's aesthetically conservative political leaders. He died by his own hand at the age of thirty-seven.

With his great gifts as a poet, graphic artist, and playwright, Vladimir Mayakovski (above) tried to reconcile the divergent aims of art and propaganda. Many critics feel that he merely prostituted his talent and ultimately became little more than a hack. Mayakovski himself was quick to acknowledge the conflict between artistic expression and political action.

Below left, a stage set painted by Mayakovski in 1919 for his **Mystery-Bouffe,** *a drama in which the "unclean" proletariat triumphs over the "clean" bourgeoisie.*

УКРАИНЦЕВ и РУСС

ДА НЕ БУДЕТ ПАН

Right, the poet Mayakovski seated at a table with Lilya Brik, the wife of the influential critic Osip Brik and a colleague of Mayakovski on the avant-garde magazine LEF *(Left Front of Art). Standing behind them are the eminent poet Boris Pasternak (left) and the film maker Sergei Eisenstein.*

Mayakovski drew this anti-White poster (left) while the Ukraine was occupied by White forces during the civil war that followed the Bolshevik seizure of power.

Above, Mayakovski's costume sketches for Mystery-Bouffe. Below, a poster by Mayakovski that was used in a Soviet campaign against anti-Semitism.

Below, a detail from a Mayakovski poster attacking counterrevolutionaries.

The First Five-Year Plan, undertaken in 1928, set unrealistic goals and called for great sacrifice from the workers. Above, a painting depicting a blast furnace in a Soviet shipyard. Left, a steel foundry in Siberia.

Below, a plow warehouse in Petrograd just after the revolution. The government hoped to replace the plows with tractors but was impeded in its efforts by the country's industrial backwardness. In the beginning, the Soviet tractor industry existed largely on propaganda posters.

lectivization. "What I saw could not be expressed in words," he wrote in his memoirs. "There was such inhuman, unimaginable misery, such terrible disaster, that it began to seem almost abstract, it would not fit within the bounds of consciousness."

Stalin's control over the party was virtually complete by the 1930s. Once-formidable rivals like Kamenev, Zinoviev, and Bukharin were by now too fearful to disagree with him openly. The USSR had become a police state. The original Bolshevik secret police, the Cheka, had been reorganized several times, first as the GPU, or State Political Administration, and then, in 1934, as the NKVD, or People's Commissariat for Internal Affairs. The NKVD exercised authority not only over the regular police but also over all prisons and labor camps.

Between 1932 and 1934, Stalin appeared to relent somewhat in his insistence on terror. He agreed, for the moment, to treat surviving kulaks more leniently, to curb the powers of the GPU, and to allow Bukharin and others to draft a new and more liberal Soviet constitution. (At the same time, though, he issued a decree holding an entire family culpable for any "treasonable" act by one of its members.) Many of these reforms had been urged on Stalin by Sergei Kirov, an old friend of Stalin's since 1909 who served as the party boss in Leningrad and had become popular enough to be seen as a potential rival. In December 1934—probably at Stalin's instigation, though it has never been proved conclusively—Kirov was killed by a terrorist. Whether or not he had planned the assassination himself, Stalin was able to use it as a pretext for a ruthless purge. More than a hundred persons were executed immediately.

Stalin then claimed that Kirov's murder had been part of a plan masterminded by the exiled Trotsky and carried out at home under the direction of Kamenev and Zinoviev. A series of spectacular show trials were held in Moscow to convince the world at large that the so-called Old Bolsheviks—the party leaders who had worked tirelessly with Lenin in the pre-1917 period and whose loyalty to the revolution was unquestionable—were in fact spies, wreckers, and counterrevolutionaries. In 1936, Kamenev, Zinoviev, and fourteen codefendants were tried publicly. To the bewilderment of the spectators in the courtroom, all "confessed" at length to the charges against them. Zinoviev and Kamenev received death sentences.

In 1937, at a second show trial, seventeen other prominent Old Bolsheviks confessed that they had been part of a plot concocted by Trotsky and the German and Japanese intelligence services. The defendants admitted to spying, conspiring to commit

In 1929 this automobile plant (above) went into operation in Nizhni Novgorod (present-day Gorkiy). Under successive Five-Year Plans, the production of heavy transport vehicles and tanks and planes was given a higher priority.

The Central Folk Art Museum sought to organize and coordinate the crafts—the "art of the people." This poster (below) proclaimed the institution to be "a friend of the shops and folk painters" and offered its assistance to craftsmen.

terrorist acts, attempting to restore capitalism in Russia, and intriguing to provoke a war against Germany in the hope of a Soviet defeat. No evidence was presented at this trial except the statements of the accused—all of whom were executed.

The final public trial took place in 1938. Twenty-one Old Bolsheviks, including Bukharin, confessed to imaginary crimes and received death sentences. Stalin thereby eliminated virtually every prominent Old Bolshevik except himself who had either known Lenin personally or been active in Lenin's circle.

How were the confessions elicited? Because the defendants in the dock showed no signs of having been physically tortured, many observers in the courtroom, including a reporter for the *New York Times,* assumed that the statements were genuine. Although the exiled Trotsky, by pointing out internal inconsistencies in the defendants' testimony, demonstrated that the charges against them were false, he was unable to explain what had motivated these strong-willed men to perjure themselves. (Trotsky himself was murdered with an ice ax by a Stalinist agent in Mexico in 1940.) It is now known that the confessions were obtained by around-the-clock interrogations coupled with promises (rarely kept) to spare the defendants' families.

With the party leadership destroyed, Stalin turned his attention to the party itself. In 1934 the party had had 2.8 million members. By 1939, Stalin had arrested fully a million of them, of whom two thirds were executed—supporters as well as opponents. Of the 139 members of the 1934 Central Committee, which had backed Stalin's purges of party leaders, 110 members, or 79 percent, were either sentenced to death or driven to suicide. Lower echelons too were devastated. Of the 1,966 delegates to the 1934 party congress, more than half were either executed or sent to labor camps. After 1939 the party congress, the Central Committee, and the Politburo rarely met, and there was no longer any pretense of party rule.

The purge of 1936–1939 affected Communist and non-Communist alike—anyone could be seized by the police. Once arrested, a prisoner would be tortured until he made out a list accusing other innocent people of crimes; then those individuals would be apprehended, and they in turn would be forced to provide other names, in an ever-widening circle of terror. In all, between seven and eight million people were arrested, of whom nearly half were shot or died from mistreatment.

Prisoners who survived interrogation were turned over to the Gulag, or Labor Camp Administration, which had established hundreds of slave-labor camps throughout the Soviet Union. In 1939 the Gulag system contained nine million prisoners. The *zeks,* as the

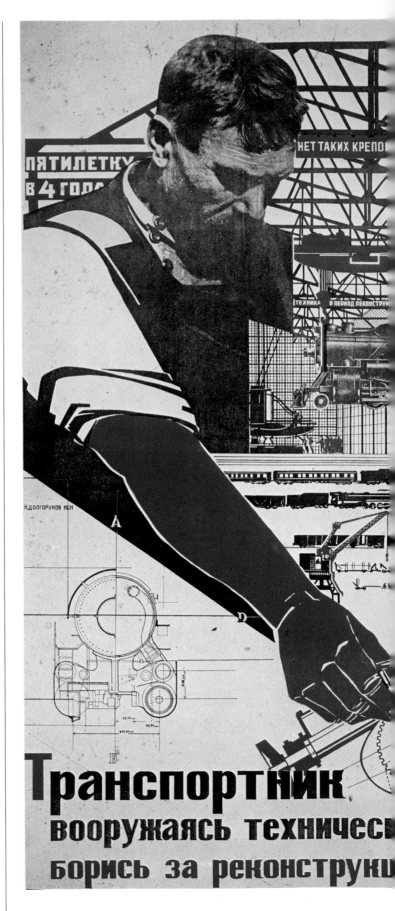

The Five-Year Plan aimed to make Soviet industry self-sufficient. The plan put factories and energy resources under the control of Gosplan, the state planning agency. Heavy industrial products were given priority over consumer goods. Above, a 1931 poster with quotations from Stalin urging transport workers to arm themselves "with technical knowledge."

The Turkestan-Siberian Railway, completed in 1930, gave the USSR a north-south line to connect with its east-west railroads. Above, construction on the railway. Right, a locomotive being refitted in the Ukraine soon after the revolution.

Once in power the Soviets denied labor unions the right to negotiate wages and to strike. Right, a 1926 poster for the Seventh Trade-Union Congress of the USSR.

"political" prisoners were called, were given little food and consigned to hard physical labor. Most died within a year or so. The novelist Aleksandr Solzhenitsyn has described this system of camps as "that amazing country of Gulag which, though scattered in an Archipelago geographically, was, in the psychological sense, fused into a continent—an almost invisible, almost imperceptible country inhabited by the zek people."

If Stalin's domestic policies were marked by cruelty, his foreign policy prior to 1939 was marked by ineptness. Stalin's provincial xenophobia, combined with his fear of socialist rivals, led him to distrust independent foreign leftists even more than he distrusted foreign capitalists. In the 1920s, over the objections of Trotsky and other Soviet leaders, he ordered the well-organized Communist Party in China to subordinate itself to the nationalist Chiang Kai-shek, who was invited to Moscow to be personally honored by the Comintern. Upon returning to China, Chiang set about executing the Communists who had dutifully obeyed Stalin's directive to put themselves under the Chinese leader's command.

In Europe, where leftists of various shades were trying to unite with moderates to prevent the rise of

Lenin's death in 1924 brought nearly half a million mourners (upper left) into the streets of Moscow in sub-zero weather to file past his casket. Immediately above, Lenin lying in state. Right, a stained-glass representation of Lenin in Moscow's Museum of the Revolution.

Hitler, Stalin declared that non-Comintern socialists were unwittingly doing more to bring about fascism than the fascists themselves. Stalin thought it best to simply stand by and let the Nazis take power in Germany, believing that this alone could convince the German people of the need for a socialist revolution. Once Hitler did assume control in 1933, all leftists were put in concentration camps. By the mid-thirties even Stalin saw the necessity for European leftists to join with moderates in a "popular front" to oppose fascism, but by then it was too late—Nazi Germany had already become a formidable military power.

In 1937, despite the likelihood of an approaching European conflict, Stalin undertook a vicious and senseless purge of the officer corps of the Red Army, whose leaders were groundlessly accused of conniving with the Germans. In secret courts-martial, sentences of death or imprisonment were handed down in the cases of two of the army's five marshals, fourteen of the army's sixteen commanders, and all of the navy's eight admirals. Corps commanders, divisional commanders, brigade commanders, and junior officers were liquidated as well. In all, some thirty-five thousand officers—about half the entire officer corps—were shot or imprisoned.

Stalin's responses to the series of diplomatic crises

Lenin's death set off a power struggle between Leon Trotsky and Joseph Stalin (right), from which Stalin eventually emerged victorious. Although few respected his theoretical abilities, Stalin was a consummate apparatchik, or party functionary. As the party's general secretary, he gained control over its party machinery and used his power to outmaneuver his better-known rival.

Below, Nadezhda Alliluyeva, Stalin's second wife, who committed suicide in 1932 after her husband publicly humiliated her at a banquet. Below right, Stalin (front row, fourth from left) watching a parade in the 1930s.

Soviet art

As commissar of education, Anatoli Lunacharski (left) was responsible for government policy on theater, film, literature, and the graphic arts.

In the first years of the Soviet regime, party leaders disagreed sharply on the issue of government control of the arts. While all thought that "counterrevolutionary" works were not to be countenanced, some, like Trotsky, felt that art has its own "peculiar laws" and argued that "the domain of art is not one in which the party is called upon to command." Other leaders insisted that only works depicting *proletkult,* or proletarian culture, should be permitted, and a few even called for the destruction of all museums and art works of the "bourgeois" past "in the name of tomorrow." Steering an often confused middle course between these extremes was Anatoli Lunacharski, the government minister responsible for exercising state control over the arts.

The brief flourishing of Soviet theater, films, and the graphic arts of the early 1920s ended abruptly later in the decade, when Stalin decried all experimental works as "formalist" and prohibited them.

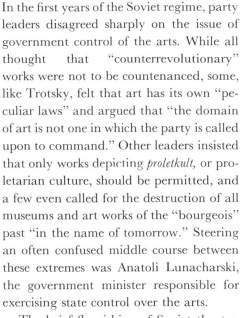

The modernist painter, designer, and architect El Lissitzky fled to Germany in the early 1920s after Lenin issued an edict against the avant-garde but returned during the winter of 1928–1929. This illustration (above) for The Story of Two Squares, *printed in 1922, shows the influence of Mondrian. Right, two Cubist-influenced prerevolutionary paintings by the Suprematist Kazimir Malevich:* The Knife Grinder *(above) and* Haymaking *(below). Such works were later denounced as "formalist" and banned.*

Under Stalin, the only permissible style was Socialist Realism, which held that the sole purpose of art was to educate the viewer in the "positive" spirit of socialism. Immediately above, Stalin and Voroshilov at the Kremlin, *by Aleksandr Gerasimov, Stalin's favorite painter.*

Above, a Cubist-influenced painted plate showing the Kremlin. Below, a carpet depicting Soviet statesman Mikhail Kalinin.

Vasili Efanov's The People Who Matter in the Land of the Soviets *(above) shows the USSR's many ethnic groups marching together in harmony in Red Square.*

Gerasimov's crude works were exalted as masterpieces by dutiful Soviet art critics. His Feast on the Kolkhoz *(right), depicting smiling picnickers gathered on a collective farm, was singled out for its "skill that cannot be derived from virtuosity but is the fruit of profound experience."*

that immediately preceded World War Two were much more sensible, even shrewd. In 1938, when Hitler threatened to occupy a portion of Czechoslovakia, the Soviet government announced that it was willing to consult with other "interested states"—that is, Britain and France—for the purposes "of checking the further development of aggression and of eliminating the increased danger of a world massacre." Whether or not Stalin was serious about joining with Britain and France to fight Germany at that time must remain a matter of speculation, because in September of that year Britain and France deliberately excluded the Soviet Union from the conference in Munich where the fate of Czechoslovakia was to be decided. The conferees agreed to partition Czechoslovakia and surrender much of it to Hitler in the hope of averting further tension. Stalin took the

After the revolution, government-owned bookstores sprang up in Moscow and Leningrad. Above, a poster by Aleksandr Rodchenko advertising books "in every branch of knowledge."

At the time of the revolution, half the Soviet population was illiterate, and education therefore became a cornerstone of the Communist program. A typical poster (top right) warned: "The illiterate is like a blind man. Failure and misfortune await him everywhere." Top left, Refresher Courses for Teachers. Above left, reading and writing courses in Soviet Central Asia. Above right, a class for women in Tashkent (south-central USSR) in the late 1920s. By 1939, eighty percent of the population could read and write. Today, illiteracy has been virtually eliminated.

ИГИ ПО ВСЕМ ОТРАСЛЯМ ЗНАНИЯ

НЕГРАМОТНЫЙ тот-же СЛЕПОЙ ВСЮДУ ЕГО ЖДУТ НЕУДАЧИ И НЕСЧАСТЬЯ

view—not unreasonably—that one intent of the Anglo-French concessions was to persuade Hitler to wage war against the USSR rather than the West. Fearful of being diplomatically isolated, Stalin soon opened his own negotiations with the Nazis.

Hitler's next logical victim was Poland, the buffer country that separated the USSR from Germany. Having capitulated to Hitler at Munich, Britain and France were now firmly pledged to go to war if Germany violated Poland's borders. Britain and France were willing to have Stalin join them in this commitment, but the Poles, whose lands had been occupied repeatedly by Russia over the centuries, refused to allow Soviet troops free passage across Polish territory to attack Germany in the event of a war. The Poles feared the Russians even more than they feared the Germans.

Anglo-French efforts to woo the USSR to their side against Germany were feeble and halfhearted. The British delegation to Moscow, for example, consisted of a group of obscure, semiretired military men, whereas Hitler sent his prominent foreign minister, Joachim von Ribbentrop. Stalin negotiated first with one side, then with the other. Finally, in August 1939, he succeeded in obtaining from Germany a ten-year nonaggression pact.

When World War Two broke out in September 1939, the USSR, in accordance with a secret protocol to the Hitler-Stalin pact, occupied eastern Poland. The Soviet Union then found itself in a position to seize the Baltic republics of Estonia, Latvia, and Lithuania, which were all annexed in August 1940. Meanwhile, Stalin moved to put Soviet industry on a full war-time footing, stepped up the production of

The USSR

"Russia is not a country, it is a world," says an old peasant proverb. The 262 million people who live in the USSR—a country that includes the Russian Soviet Federated Socialist Republic (RSFSR) and fourteen other Soviet republics—are members of more than a hundred distinct ethnic groups and speak about two hundred dif-

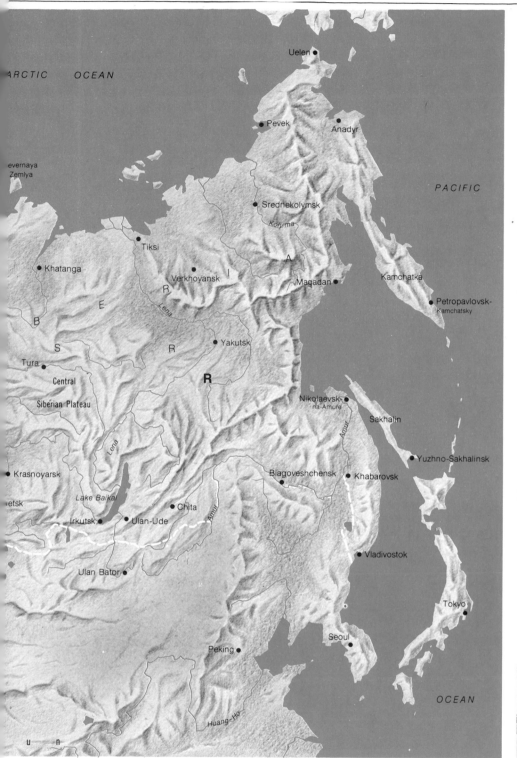

ferent languages and dialects. Seventy-five percent of the inhabitants—primarily Russians, Ukrainians, and Byelorussians—live in the western USSR and speak Slavic languages. In the southern USSR, including parts of the Volga basin, the Caucasus, the Crimea, and much of central Asia, Turkic and Tatar peoples predominate.

The USSR, which occupies more than a seventh of the earth's land surface, extends some 6,800 miles from east to west and some 2,800 miles from north to south. It stretches from the barren tundra above the Arctic Circle across the densely forested taiga and fertile steppes of the central regions to the arid deserts of the south. A visitor to the various capitals of the USSR's constituent republics will be struck more by the cities' differences than by their similarities. Each has its own architecture, customs, and street life. Facing page (from top): Tallinn, in the Estonian SSR; Vilnius, in the Lithuanian SSR; Kiev, in the Ukrainian SSR; and Moscow, in the RSFSR. This page (from top): Minsk, in the Byelorussian SSR; Yerevan, in the Armenian SSR; Tashkent, in the Uzbek SSR; and Riga, in the Latvian SSR.

Grigori Ordzhonikidze

Grigori Zinoviev

Nikolai Bukharin

Lev Kamenev

Karl Radek   Mikhail Tukhachevski   Aleksei Rykov

The more prominent victims of Stalin's terror were kept in Moscow's grim Lubyanka Prison (top right), where they were interrogated without sleep for days on end until they broke down and agreed to "confess" publicly to crimes they had never committed. After their trials, which were conducted by Stalin's ruthless chief prosecutor Andrei Vyshinsky (center), the defendants were returned to the Lubyanka and executed with a pistol shot in the back of the head. Above, a prison for political detainees in the Siberian city of Novosibirsk. Left, seven victims of the purges. Facing page, below right, the Politburo of 1936, which approved the purges.

The purges

In 1934 one of Stalin's loyal henchmen in the Communist Party, Sergei Kirov, was assassinated by a terrorist, possibly on Stalin's orders. After the murder, Stalin proclaimed Kirov a martyred national hero and carried his cremated remains in a memorial procession (above left). Announcing later that the killing had been part of a conspiracy masterminded from abroad by the exiled Leon Trotsky (above), Stalin used the incident as a pretext for arresting all his former rivals still in the USSR. Three spectacular show trials were held in Moscow, during which virtually every prominent "Old Bolshevik" who had known Lenin confessed publicly to imaginary crimes. By 1939 more than a million people had been arrested, of whom two thirds were sentenced to death. "To choose one's victims," Stalin once confided to an associate, "to prepare one's plans minutely, to slake an implacable vengeance, and then to go to bed ... there is nothing sweeter in the world."

tanks and planes, and began rebuilding the Red Army.

The need for a military reorganization became apparent during a short territorial war against Finland in the winter of 1940–1941. The fighting was expected to last ten or twelve days; instead, the greatly outnumbered Finns held out for more than three months and inflicted more than two hundred thousand casualties. The inexperience of the Soviet field commanders, the lack of coordination between various branches of the Red Army, and the incompetence of the overall command in ordering suicidal massed frontal attacks against entrenched positions did not go unnoticed by Hitler.

In 1941, unable to mount an amphibious invasion of England, Hitler decided to turn eastward, against his Soviet ally. Although the German general staff doubted the wisdom of embroiling Germany in a war on two fronts, Hitler was sure the Red Army could be destroyed quickly in a short campaign. He told his generals: "You only have to kick in the door and the whole rotten structure will come tumbling down." Allied intelligence services learned of the impending attack and warned Stalin, but Stalin assumed that the Allies were merely scheming to draw the USSR into the war for their own ends. Although Stalin had

Sergei Eisenstein

The extraordinary films of Sergei Eisenstein (1898–1948) lifted the fledgling Soviet film industry into the forefront of world cinema. For *The Battleship Potemkin* (1925), he used a new editing technique called montage to depict a famous naval mutiny of 1905 in a striking series of rapidly changing images and close-ups. The same technique distinguished *October* (1928), a gripping propagandistic account of the 1917 revolution. In the 1930s, with his montage theories under attack by Stalin as "formalist," Eisenstein emigrated to the United States, but he found Hollywood even more stifling than Stalin. Returning to his homeland in 1933, he publicly excoriated himself for his former aesthetic heresies. During the last decade of his life, he directed *Alexander Nevsky* and *Ivan the Terrible,* which stand alongside *Potemkin* as cinematic masterpieces.

Eisenstein left nothing to chance in his work. Long before filming began, he carefully designed each shot to ensure that once production was under way every camera angle and close-up would contribute to his overall plan. Above, a preparatory sketch for Ivan the Terrible, Part I *(1944). Right, Eisenstein posing for a photograph on the set of* Old and New *(1929), a lyrical tribute to collectivization in the countryside.*

Facing page, a director and his films. Above and below far left, two scenes from The Battleship Potemkin. Above and below center, Eisenstein during the shooting of Old and New and Que Viva Mexico! (1931–1932), an American-financed film that was never completed. Above right, a scene from Ivan the Terrible, Part II (1946). Below right, a scene from the propagandistic October.

After his disastrous experiences in Hollywood, Eisenstein returned to the USSR, recanted his former "formalist" theories of montage, and developed an entirely new style for Alexander Nevsky (1938), a large-budget, epic sound film with a score by Sergei Prokofiev. Above left, Nikolai Cherkasov in the title role. The film's climactic battle scene (above right) was almost operatic in its stately formality.

In Ivan the Terrible (top center and right), which also featured Cherkasov, Eisenstein carried his operatic style even further: The scenes are visually static; the actors hardly move. The director had to modify his original themes midway through production because of fluctuations in Stalin's attitude toward the historical Ivan. Below, posters advertising films by various Soviet directors.

In August 1939, on the eve of World War Two, the Soviets signed a ten-year nonaggression pact with Germany (above). Stalin is shown looking on at the extreme right.

no illusions about Hitler's ultimate intentions toward the USSR, he was convinced that Germany would not act as long as Britain remained in the war.

When the attack came, at three in the morning on June 22, 1941, Soviet frontier soldiers were taken almost completely by surprise. Within hours, three Soviet infantry divisions were annihilated and five others were cut to pieces. By the second day, two thousand Soviet planes had been destroyed, many of them on the ground. Three million Wehrmacht soldiers marched across the USSR along a two-thousand-mile front. Stalin had made no plans whatever for a defensive retreat; bridges and rail installations were captured intact by the Germans.

During these crucial days, the country was leaderless. Stalin himself, according to his subordinate Nikita Khrushchev, was suffering from a nervous breakdown. Only on June 30 did he regain enough mental presence to begin issuing directives. Three days later, he addressed the Soviet people by radio—his first public pronouncement since the outbreak of the war. One Soviet ambassador described Stalin's voice as "dull" and "colorless" during the broadcast, as if he were "at the end of his strength."

While Stalin struggled to piece together a command structure, the Red Army continued to give way before the Wehrmacht. The Ukraine, the granary of the USSR, was in enemy hands by the end of October. The invading Nazis took some three million Soviet prisoners of war, and about sixty-five million Soviet civilians—forty percent of the country's population—lived under German occupation. The Germans also controlled more than half of the Soviet Union's pig-iron, steel, and aluminum output and forty-one percent of its railroad lines. The leading panzer divisions of the German army advanced all the way to the outskirts of Leningrad and Moscow before bogging down in the early winter snows. In 1942 a German force drove into the southern USSR. To keep vital industrial installations out of German hands, the Soviets were forced to dismantle entire factories and ship them east to Siberia.

In September 1939, Soviet and German troops invaded Poland. This page, center, fraternization between the two occupying armies. Later in the year, the USSR attacked Finland but suffered heavy casualties at the hands of the Finnish ski troops (left).

The Red Army's poor performance against Finland was one of the considerations that led Hitler, in June 1941, to launch a sudden attack against the USSR. Facing page, below left and below center, Soviet civilian refugees fleeing before the German onslaught.

Within a few months, German forces penetrated deep into the USSR. Above, German troops on the road to Moscow. Wehrmacht soldiers (near left) march through a bombed-out Soviet village. Below, a Soviet railway station just after a German air attack.

Propaganda

The sudden growth of the mass media in the first decades of the twentieth century—radio, motion-picture newsreels, magazine and newspaper photography—was exploited by the propaganda ministries of totalitarian and democratic governments alike. Hitler, who had admired Britain's propaganda efforts in World War One, saw to it that his shrewd minister Joseph Goebbels exercised complete control over the German press, radio, cinema, and theater. Similarly, Stalin kept a tight rein on all the Soviet media. In the early stages of World War Two, he attempted to rally the Soviet people under the banner of Communism, but when this failed he began appealing instead to his subjects' nationalism—and, ironically, to their religious beliefs.

In April 1943 the Germans announced that the bodies of some 4,250 Polish officers had been uncovered in a mass grave in the Katyn forest near Smolensk (in the western USSR) and attributed the massacre to Soviet troops. Above, a German poster showing Soviet troops carrying out the executions. A postwar American investigation confirmed that the victims had been murdered by Stalin's secret police.

In their efforts to win over the Soviet people, Nazi propagandists accompanying the invading German armies boasted in Russian-language posters (below left) of a "New Order" in Europe. Below, a Nazi poster in which Winston Churchill and Stalin are depicted as allies in a "Jewish conspiracy against Europe." Above, a Soviet caricature of Italy, a Nazi ally until 1943, torn apart by the war.

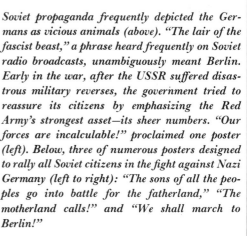

НАШИ СИЛЫ НЕИСЧИСЛИМЫ

Soviet propaganda frequently depicted the Germans as vicious animals (above). "The lair of the fascist beast," a phrase heard frequently on Soviet radio broadcasts, unambiguously meant Berlin. Early in the war, after the USSR suffered disastrous military reverses, the government tried to reassure its citizens by emphasizing the Red Army's strongest asset—its sheer numbers. "Our forces are incalculable!" proclaimed one poster (left). Below, three of numerous posters designed to rally all Soviet citizens in the fight against Nazi Germany (left to right): "The sons of all the peoples go into battle for the fatherland," "The motherland calls!" and "We shall march to Berlin!"

РОДИНА-МАТЬ ЗОВЕТ!

ВОЕННАЯ ПРИСЯГА

ДОЙДЕМ ДО БЕРЛИНА!

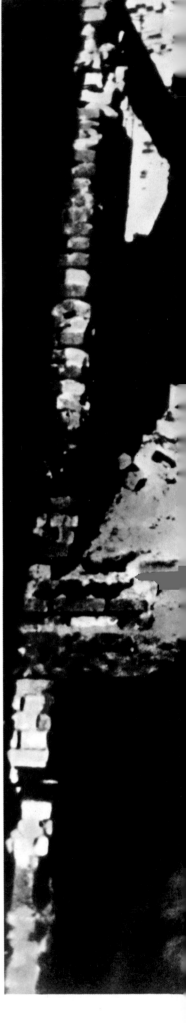

Although preoccupied with the war effort, Stalin also found time to intensify his dictatorial grip on the USSR. On May 6, 1941, a month and a half before the Germans attacked, he had become chairman of the Council of Commissars—the first official government post he had claimed for himself since 1922. He now ruled the USSR in name as well as fact. Stalin's first act upon recovering from the nervous collapse brought on by the war was to form a State Defense Committee "uniting in its hands the plenitude of state powers," of which he was to serve as chairman. Two weeks later he became commissar of defense, and on August 7 commander in chief of the armed forces.

In the first years of the war—before he learned to leave his generals alone—Stalin's military strategy was often questionable and sometimes disastrous. Particularly damaging was his refusal to allow outnumbered Soviet armies to fall back and regroup at more defensible positions. "Not a single step backward. . . . You have to fight to your last drop of blood to defend every position, every foot of Soviet territory," a typical order of the day read. Generals whose armies were about to be surrounded and cut off by the Germans pleaded with Stalin for permission to retreat, but he invariably denied the request. As a result, entire army groups were needlessly sacrificed.

With large areas of the USSR under German occupation, Soviet civilians formed partisan units to harass enemy supply routes. By 1943, ten percent of all German divisions in the USSR were engaged in the fight against partisans. This page, top, the execution of a young Ukrainian partisan.

The failure in early 1943 of the German attack against Stalingrad (right), on the Volga River, marked the turning point of the war in Russia. The Germans, under the command of General Friedrich Paulus, lost some three hundred thousand men. Above, "Defend Mother Volga," a Soviet propaganda poster. Above left, a painting showing the burial of a Soviet officer at the front.

Though ordered by Hitler to fight on at Stalingrad "to the last man and the last bullet," General Paulus (above) surrendered his Sixth Army on February 2, 1943. Right, the surrender by Paulus.

Generals who did give ground, however sensible their reasons, were summoned to Moscow and shot. Soldiers in encircled units who were taken prisoner by the Germans faced prosecution as traitors after the war.

Initially, Stalin attempted to rally the Soviet people under the banner of communism, but when that proved ineffective he dropped the socialist slant in government propaganda and instead appealed to his subjects' nationalism. The slogan on the masthead of *Pravda* was changed from "Workers of the world, unite!" to "Death to the German invader!" To replace the "Internationale," the hymn of international socialism, Stalin commissioned a national anthem, which praised "Great Russia"—and Stalin himself. In 1943, he dissolved the Comintern.

Eventually, as the German army found itself mired in the mud and its supply lines overextended, the tide turned. No matter how many Soviet soldiers the Germans killed, more kept coming. "In fighting the Russians," a Wehrmacht colonel wrote in a letter home,

Georgi Zhukov (below), one of the few Soviet generals Stalin trusted, led the successful Red Army defense of Moscow in 1941 and planned the encirclement of the German forces at Stalingrad in 1943. He later commanded the Red Army offensives against Germany that resulted in the capture of Berlin in April 1945. Soviet-built Katyusha missiles (above) aided the Red Army victory. Right, Soviet troops recapturing Petrodvorets, a former czarist summer residence.

"the German Army is like an elephant attacking a host of ants. The elephant will kill thousands—maybe millions—but in the end their numbers will overcome him, and he will be eaten to the bone." In February 1943, the German forces outside Stalingrad were encircled by the Red Army and destroyed. During the next two years, the Soviets slowly pushed the Germans back to Berlin, occupying Bulgaria, Hungary, Romania, and Poland in the process.

German bombing, combined with the Soviets' own scorched-earth policy of leaving nothing of economic value salvageable in areas about to be occupied by the enemy, resulted in the destruction of 1,710 cities, 70,000 villages, 32,000 industrial facilities, 98,000 kolkhozes, 1,876 sovkhozes, 40,000 miles of railroad track, 84,000 schools, and most of the bridges, hospitals, and libraries in the Germans' path. The human cost was even greater—twenty million Soviet citizens lost their lives.

Stalin took full credit for the victory. In the newspapers, on radio, and in newsreels he was portrayed as the guiding military genius behind the Red Army's success. Having achieved absolute dictatorial power over the Soviet Union, he now sought to gain control of history. Soviet historians dutifully wrote treatises glorifying his early work in the party, his struggles against such traitors as Trotsky and Bukharin, and his wise insistence on collectivization and forced industrialization—which, in the official Soviet view, had enabled the USSR to build enough tanks and planes to win the war. Even the humiliating defeats of the first years of the war were extolled as proof of Stalin's military genius. These apparent setbacks were held to have been a part of a deliberate and innovative "counteroffensive" strategy to lure the German forces deep into Soviet territory so that they could be more easily destroyed.

The war also served to enhance Stalin's position on the world stage. At the Allied conference at Teheran in 1943, he had met with President Franklin Delano Roosevelt and Prime Minister Winston Churchill and had been treated by them—and by the American and British press, which referred to him as a benign

"Uncle Joe"—as a great statesman. In fact, Stalin, through a combination of charm and bullying, was probably the most successful of the three negotiators. He persuaded his new friends that after the war eastern Poland should come within the "sphere of influence" of the Soviet Union. In another meeting, at the Soviet resort city of Yalta early in 1945, Stalin was quite agreeable to the proposition that free elections should be permitted in the countries of eastern Europe that were occupied by the Red Army.

The free elections never took place. Instead, puppet regimes loyal to Stalin were installed by various coercive means. Within a few years, Albania, Bulgaria, Czechoslovakia, East Germany, Hungary, Poland, and Romania were all in Stalin's hands. The Soviet Union, which since its inception had felt itself surrounded on all sides by hostile capitalist governments, had at last achieved a degree of international stability and safety—not through proletarian revolution, as Lenin and Trotsky had hoped, but as a result of a world war. The Soviet Union had become a full-fledged world power, second only to the United States.

Photography Credits

American Museum of Natural History, N.Y.: p. 43, pp. 54–55 top center / *Arborio-Mella:* p. 24 top, p. 58 center, pp. 70–71 / *Bildarchiv Preussischer Kulturbesitz:* p. 117 center right / *Campeggi:* p. 81 top right / *Costa:* p. 15 top, p. 17 center right, p. 19, p. 20 bottom, p. 22 bottom, p. 23 bottom, p. 28, p. 29 first from top, p. 33 center left, p. 42 center, p. 50, p. 51, p. 56 top, p. 57 bottom, p. 60, p. 65 top right, p. 66, p. 67, p. 72 top, p. 75 top left, p. 78 top left, p. 79 bottom right, p. 85 bottom left, p. 93 center left, bottom right, and left, p. 100 top left, p. 103 top left, right, and center right, p. 106, p. 107 left, p. 109 center, p. 111 bottom right, p. 115 bottom right, p. 121 bottom right, p. 126 bottom, p. 128 bottom, p. 130 left bottom, p. 131 top right, p. 140 bottom, p. 141 right, p. 143 bottom left and bottom right, pp. 152–153 center, p. 153 top right, p. 159 bottom center and right / *Costa-Gussani:* p. 117 top, p. 148 right / *Arch. De Cesare:* pp. 124–125 top center, p. 126 top / *Dilia-Neubert:* p. 134 bottom left, p. 135 top / *Dulevant:* p. 119 top / *Archivio Fabbri:* p. 34 top, p. 48 top left, p. 54 bottom left and right, p. 55 top, p. 64 bottom left, p. 69 bottom left, p. 73 bottom left, p. 74 top, p. 76 bottom right, p. 80 top left, p. 89, p. 90 bottom, p. 107 top right, p. 117 bottom left, p. 121 left, p. 137 top left, p. 140 top, p. 145 bottom, p. 146, p. 147 bottom, p. 150 center and bottom left / *Facetti:* p. 58 bottom left, p. 59 center left and right / *Fossati-Salmi:* p. 96 bottom left and right, p. 108 top left, right, center, and bottom, p. 110 top, p. 111 top right / *Foto 2000:* p. 108 center right, p. 109 bottom and top, p. 118 top / *Robert Hunt Library:* p. 96 top left / *Keystone:* p. 120 bottom / *Magnum-R. Capa:* p. 157 top right / *Magnum-Glinn:* p. 136 top / *Magnum-Haas:* pp. 52–53 center, p. 72 center / *Magnum-Lessing:* p. 24 bottom center, p. 25 center, p. 35 right, p. 38 top left, p. 39 top, p.137 top right / *Magnum-Morath:* p. 10 center / *Magnum-Stock:* p. 77 top / *Mairani:* p. 9, p. 21 top, p. 30 bottom left, p. 33 center right and bottom right, p. 59 bottom right, p. 75 top center and bottom / *Marka:* p. 52 top left, p. 61 top left, p. 85 bottom right, p. 134 top left / *Marka-Giaretti:* p. 72 bottom right / *Marka-G. Heilman:* p. 10 top and bottom, p. 11 top and bottom left, p. 45 bottom, p. 53 top right and bottom right / *Marka-Mauri:* p. 154 bottom / *Marka-Myers:* p. 42 top / *Marka-Jack Novak:* p. 11 bottom right / *Marka-Photri:* p. 36 bottom right, p. 37 bottom left and right / *Marka-Wilson:* p. 37 top left / *Arch. Moro:* p. 87, pp. 90–91 top center, p. 91 center, bottom left, and right, p. 92, p. 93 top, p. 101 left, p. 102, p. 104 bottom left, top right, and bottom, p. 108 center left, p. 113 right, p. 117 bottom right, p. 129 right, p. 138 top, p. 142 bottom left, p. 151 top right / *Museum of the American Indian, N.Y.:* p. 12 / *National Portrait Gallery, London:* p. 13 bottom right / *NIL-Facetti:* pp. 150–151 bottom center / *N.Y. Historical Society:* p. 15 bottom left, p. 41 top left, p. 47, p. 48 top right and bottom / *Novosti:* p. 91 top right, p. 94 top and bottom left, p. 95 top right and bottom, p. 98, p. 99, p. 100 bottom, p. 110 bottom, p. 112 top left and right, p. 112 bottom left and center right, p. 113, p. 116 top, p. 118 bottom, second, third, and fourth from left, p. 119 bottom, first from left, and bottom last three pictures on right, p. 122, p. 123 top, pp. 124–125 bottom center, p. 125 top right and bottom, p. 126 center, p. 127 bottom, p. 134 top right and bottom right, p. 135 bottom left and right, p. 136 bottom, pp. 136–137 top center, p. 137 bottom, pp. 138–139 bottom center, p. 139 bottom center and top left, p. 144, p. 145 top, p. 147 top and center, p. 148 top left and bottom, p. 151 right center, p. 152 bottom left, p. 153 bottom right, p. 154, second from top, p. 155 second from top and bottom, p. 158 bottom left and right, p. 163 top left, p. 164 left, p. 165 left and bottom right, p. 166 top and bottom left / *D. Pellegrini:* p. 52 bottom, p. 53 bottom left, p. 72 bottom left / *L. Pellegrini:* p. 120 top left / *M. Pellegrini:* p. 75 top right / *Photri:* p. 14 top and bottom right, p. 29, third and fourth from top, p. 57, first three pictures from top, p. 61 center left, p. 65 bottom, p. 73 center, p. 74 bottom, p. 77 bottom / *P. Popper:* p. 115 top, p. 156 left, second from top / *Publifoto:* p. 82 center right, p. 83 bottom right, p. 118 bottom, last on right, p. 129 top left, p. 130 top left, p. 156 left, first, third, fourth, and fifth from top, p. 156 bottom, top right, and center right / *Pucciarelli:* pp. 12–13 center, p. 103 bottom, p. 104 top left, p. 105, pp. 130–131 top center, p. 150 bottom right, p. 152 top left / *Ricciarini:* pp. 62–63 / *Lores Riva:* p. 16 bottom, p. 17 top right, p. 18 top left, p. 22 top right, p. 23 top, p. 30 center left, p. 31 bottom left, p. 32 bottom, p. 55 center, p. 61 bottom left, p. 64 bottom right, p. 69 top, p. 73 top, p. 80 bottom right, p. 82 bottom, p. 83 top right, p. 101 right, p. 115 bottom left, p. 116 bottom, p. 121 top right, p. 128 top, p. 129 left, center, and bottom, p. 131 bottom right, p. 141 left top and bottom, p. 142 top and bottom right, pp. 142–143 top center, p. 143 top right, p. 158 top, p. 159 top and bottom left, p. 162, p. 163 top right and bottom, p. 164 top right and bottom / *Rizzoli:* p. 15 bottom right, pp. 16–17 top center, p. 18 bottom right, p. 24 bottom left, p. 30 top left, p. 31 top, p. 33 top, p. 36 top, p. 40 bottom, p. 44 top left and bottom, p. 80 top right, p. 81 top left and center, p. 82 top right and top left, p. 83 left and center right, p. 94 bottom right, p. 95 top left, p. 96 top right, p. 97, p. 100 top right and center left, p. 107 bottom right, p. 112 bottom right, p. 114 bottom, p. 118 bottom, first from left, p. 119 bottom, second from left, p. 127 top, p. 149 bottom left, p. 150 top, p. 156 center left, p. 157 top left, p. 160 top and bottom, p. 165 top right, p. 166 bottom right, p. 167 / *Roger-Viollet:* p. 120 top right / *Scala:* p. 114 top, pp. 132–133, p. 138 bottom, pp. 150–151 top center, p. 151 bottom right / *SEF:* p. 13 top right, p. 14 bottom left, p. 20 top, p. 21 bottom, p. 31 bottom right, p. 32 top and center, p. 33 bottom left, p. 34 bottom, p. 35 left, p. 36 bottom left, p. 38 top right and bottom, p. 39 bottom, p. 40 top, p. 41 bottom left and top right, p. 42 bottom, p. 44 top right and center, p. 45 top, p. 46 bottom left, p. 49, p. 55 bottom right, p. 64 top left, p. 68, p. 69 bottom right, p. 73 bottom right, p. 76 top and bottom left, p. 84 top left and bottom, p. 85 top, p. 154 top and third from top, p. 155 top and third from top / *Starfoto-Zefa:* pp. 110–111 center / *Stern:* p. 160 center / *Team Editorial:* p. 149 top and bottom right, p. 157 bottom / *Titus:* p. 18 top right and bottom left / *Ullstein Bilderdienst:* p. 123 bottom / *Ullstein-Grimm:* p. 161 top and top center / *Ullstein-P. Wolff und Trifschler:* p. 161 bottom left, bottom center, and bottom right / *S. Visalli:* p. 17 bottom left and right, p. 18 bottom center, p. 22 top left, p. 25 bottom and top, p. 29, second from top, p. 37 top right, p. 38 bottom left, p. 46 top, center left, right, bottom left, and center, p. 58 top left and right, p. 59 top left, right, and bottom left, p. 61 top right and bottom, p. 64 center left, p. 78 top right, center, and bottom, p. 79 left, top right, and center, p. 80 center top, p. 81 bottom left, center right, and bottom

Cover photo courtesy of the Harry T. Peters Collection, Museum of the City of New York

Index

abolitionists, 64–68
Adams, John, *29, 34,* 41, 45, 48
Adams, John Quincy, *42*
Adams, Samuel, 32
advertising, 46, *46*
agriculture
    cotton in, *60, 61*
    of plains (US), 81
    Soviet, collectivization of, *136–137, 137–145,* 167
    Soviet, in famine of 1920s, *128–129*
    Soviet, peasants in, 124–128
    tobacco in, *13, 20,* 21
Alamo, Battle of the, *44,* 60
Alaska, 72, *72,* 86
Albania, 168
Allen, Ethan, 39
Alliluyeva, Nadezhda, *149*
All-Russian Congress of Soviets, 109, *125*
America
    Anglo-French wars in, 29–31
    British colonies in, 31–32
    settlement of, 12–13, 19–29
    see also United States
American Federation of Labor, 85
American Revolution, *17,* 21–23, *29–31,* 32–41
Amherst, Jeffrey, *16*
Andros, Sir Edmund, 23, 29
Anthony, Susan B., 86
Antietam, battle of, *68*
Apache Indians, *76,* 81
apparatchiks, 122, *149*
Appomattox (Virginia), 13, *69, 75*
architecture
    of Kremlin, *134–135,* 135
    of Monticello, 36, *36–37*
armies
    in American Revolution, *21–23,* 38–41
    in Anglo-French wars in America, 30–31
    Bolshevik, *123*
    British, in America, 31–38
    czarist, in World War One, *108, 110*
    German, in World War One, *109*
    German, in World War Two, *160–162, 164–165*
    Red, Kronstadt rebellion suppressed by, 118
    Red, Stalin's purge of, *149*
    Red, under Trotsky, *126, 127*
    Red, Trotsky removed as head of, 131
    Red, in World War Two, 157–167, *163, 166*
    Russian, in Revolution of 1917, 103–104, *115*
    in Russian civil war, 111–114, *130, 143*
    US, in Mexican War, 60
    US, in Spanish-American War, *84,* 86
    in US Civil War, *64, 66–68,* 69, *69,* 75
Arnold, Benedict, 39–41
art
    of Eisenstein's films, 158, *158–159*
    Soviet, 150, *150–151*
    Soviet, Mayakovski and, 142, *142–143*
Articles of Confederation (1781), 43
Aurora (cruiser), *121*
Austria, in World War One, *110*
Azores, 15–16

Bacon, Nathaniel, Jr., 21
Balabanov, Angelica, 116
Baltimore and Ohio Railroad, *59*
Bank of the United States, 45, 57
Bartholdi, Frédéric, *10*
Beauregard, Pierre G.T. de, 69
Belgium, 94
Belvedere Palace (Kremlin, Moscow), *135*
Bemis, Samuel Flagg, 13
Berkeley, Sir William, 21

Berlin, Soviet capture of, *166,* 167
blacks
    in post-Civil War US, 77–80
    in twentieth-century US, 86
    in Union army, 69
    see also slavery and slaves
Bogdanov, Aleksandr, *118*
Bolsheviks, 95–102, 104, 107–116, *116, 117, 121*
    early leadership of, *118–119*
    opposition to, *122*
    purge trials of, 145–146, *156,* 157
Boone, Daniel, *16*
Booth, John Wilkes, *74*
Boscawen, Edward, *16*
Boston (Massachusetts), *39*
    in American Revolution, *23,* 35–39
Boston Massacre, *18,* 32
Boston Tea Party, *20, 21,* 35
Bottridge, Jenneus, *48*
Braddock, Edward, 30–31
Breed's Hill, battle of, *23,* 39
Brest Litovsk, Treaty of (1917), 110–111, *127*
Brik, Lilya, *142*
Britain (England)
    American colonies of, *13,* 19–29
    American Revolution and, *22, 23, 29–31,* 32–41
    Boston Tea Party and, *20, 21*
    in French and Indian War, *16, 17,* 30–31
    Monroe Doctrine and, 60
    New World exploration by, 16
    post-Revolutionary US and, 45, 48
    in pre-World War Two period, 152–153, 160
    in Russian civil war, 114
    Stamp Act in, *18*
    in War of 1812, *41,* 52
    in World War One, 88
    World War One propaganda of, 162
British East India Company, 35
Brooklyn Bridge (New York), *80*
Brooks, Preston, 65
Brown, John, 68
Bubnov, Andrei, *118*
buffalo, 54, *55*
Bukharin, Nikolai, 111, 122, 128, 131, 136, 145, 167
    purge trial of, 146, *156*
Bulgaria, 167, 168
Bunker Hill, Battle of, *23, 39*
Burgoyne, John, 40
Burr, Aaron, *34*

Cabot, John, 16
Cabot, Sebastian, 16
Calhoun, John C., *61*
California
    ceded to US by Mexico, 60
    gold rush in, *16, 18,* 64, 72, *72–73*
Calvinists, 21
Camden (South Carolina), battle of, 41
Cameron, Simon, 77
Canada
    invaded by US, 52
    lost to Britain by France, 31
    Quebec Act and, 35
    Treaty of Paris (1783) and, 43
Capitol building (Washington, D.C.), *48*
Carnegie, Andrew, 81, *81*
Cartier, Jacques, *12*
Cathedral of the Annunciation (Kremlin, Moscow), *134,* 135
Catt, Carrie Chapman, 86
Cedar Creek, battle of, *66*
Central Folk Art Museum, *145*
Central Pacific Railroad, 59, *59,* 80
Chancellorsville, battle of, *66*
Charles I (king, England), 22
Charles II (king, England), 21
Charleston (South Carolina), 40
Chattanooga, battle of, *66*
Cheka (Soviet secret police), 116, 145
Cherkasov, Nikolai, *159*
Cherokee Indians, 57
chess, 112
Chiang Kai-shek, 148

China
    Communist Party in, 148
    US "Open Door" policy toward, 88
Choctaw Indians, *54*
Churchill, Winston, 106, 114, *162,* 167–168, *167*
Church of the Nativity (Kremlin, Moscow), *134*
civil war (Russia), 111–114, *130, 143*
    Trotsky and, *126*
Civil War (US), 13, *64,* 69–76
    battles of, *66–67*
Clark, George Rogers, *17,* 41
Clark, William, 38
class structure
    of American colonies, 21
    Soviet, peasants in, 124–128
    Soviet executions and, 116
Clay, Henry, 52
Clinton, Henry, 40
Coercive Acts (Intolerable Acts; 1774), 35
Columbus, Christopher, 9, 16
Comintern (Communist International; Third International), 120
commerce
    of New York City, *50, 51,* 57
    of post-Revolutionary US, 45–48
    railroads and, 58–59, 81
    regulation of (US), 84, 86
    between Soviet Union and West, 120–121
    in US, 14–15
    under War Communism, 116
Communist Party (China), 148
Communist Party (USSR), 97
    Bolshevik leadership of, *118–119*
    Comintern under control of, 120
    after Lenin's death, 124–131
    Stalin's purges in, 145–148, *156,* 157
    structure of, 122
Compromise of 1850 (US), 64
Concord (Massachusetts), 35
    battle of, *23,* 38
Confederate States of America, *64,* 68–75
    surrender of, *69*
Conkling, Roscoe, 77
Connecticut, 23
Constitution, US, 43–45
    Thirteenth Amendment (abolition of slavery) to, 75
    Fourteenth Amendment to (Reconstruction Amendment), 76
Constitutional Convention (1785), 24, *25*
Continental Congress, 35, 38, 43
Cooper, James Fenimore, 53
Cornwallis, Charles, *31,* 41
cotton, 57, *60, 61*
Council of People's Commissars, 110
Crazy Horse (Sioux chief), 80
Crockett, Davy, *44*
Cuba, *84,* 86, 88
currency
    Confederate, *64*
    Soviet, *140*
Currier, Nathaniel, *72*
Custer, George A., *75,* 80
Czechoslovakia, 152, 168

Davenport, John, 23
Davis, Jefferson, *64,* 68
Dawes, William, *21*
Dawes Severalty Act (US, 1887), 54
Declaration of Independence (1776), 10, *29,* 40
Declaration of Rights (1774), 35
democratic centrism, 97
Democratic Republicans, 38, 45
Dewey, George, 86–88
Douglas, Stephen A., 65
Douglass, Frederick, *61*
Dred Scott case (1857), 65
Dubasov, Fëdor, *102*
DuBois, William E.B., 86
Duma (Russian general assembly), 98, *101, 102,* 104, *115*
Dutch West India Company, 29
Dzerzhinski, Feliks, *118*
Dzhugashvili, Joseph, *see* Stalin, Joseph

Eakins, Thomas, *76*
East Germany, 168
Eastman, George, *81*
Eaton, Theophilus, 23
economy
  Russian, in 1917, 109
  Soviet, industrialization debate in, 124–128
  Soviet, NEP and, 118–121, 138
  Soviet, in 1920s, *128, 140*
  Soviet, under Stalin, 136–145, *144–147*
Edison, Mina, *78*
Edison, Thomas A., 78, *78–79*
Efanov, Vasili, *151*
Eisenstein, Sergei, *142,* 158, *158–159*
electrification
  Edison and, 78, *78–79*
  in Soviet Union, 138, *138–139*
Elizabeth I (queen, England), *13,* 19
Ellis Island (New York), *82*
Emancipation Proclamation (1863), *64,* 69
Embargo Act (US, 1807), 48
Emerson, Ralph Waldo, 57
England, *see* Britain
Erie Canal (New York), *48, 50,* 57
Estonia, 153

Federalists, 38, 45, 52
Ferdinand V (the Catholic; king, Castile), 16
films, of Eisenstein, 158, *158–159*
Finland, 157, *160*
Five Forks, battle of, *67,* 75
Five-Year Plans, 136, 137, *144–146*
flags, US, *22*
Florida, 31, *43*
  sold to US by Spain, *42,* 57
Ford, Henry, 84
Fort Frontenac (Canada), 31
Fort Monmouth, battle of, 40
Fort Pillow, battle of, *67*
Fort Sumter, battle of, *64,* 69
Fort Ticonderoga, battle of, *39,* 40
France
  American Revolution and, 40, 41
  Franklin in, 24
  in French and Indian War, *16, 17,* 30–31
  Louisiana Territory sold to US by, 38, 48
  New World exploration by, 16
  in pre-World War Two period, 152–153
  Revolution in, 45
  Statue of Liberty given to US by, *10*
  in World War One, 88
Franklin, Benjamin, 24, *24–25,* 29, 30, 32, 40, 41
Franklin, William, *24*
Franklin (Tennessee), battle of, *66*
Fredericksburg, battle of, *66*
French and Indian War, *16, 17,* 30–31
French Revolution (1789), 45
Fugitive Slave Act (US, 1850), 64
Fuller, Margaret, 65

Gadsden, Christopher, 32
Gadsden Purchase, 60
Gage, Thomas, 35–39
Gates, Horatio, 40, 41
George III (king, England), *18, 29, 39*
Gerasimov, Aleksandr, *150, 151*
Germany
  under Hitler, 149–153
  Lenin's trip through, 105–106, *118*
  revolutionary socialist movement in, 121
  Treaty of Brest Litovsk and, 110–111, *127*
  in World War One, 88, *109, 110*
  in World War Two, 153–167, *160–161, 164, 166*
  World War Two propaganda and, 162, *162–163*
Geronimo (Apache chief), *76,* 81
Gettysburg, battle of, *67*
Ghent, Treaty of (1814), 52
Goebbels, Joseph, 162
gold rush
  in California (1849), *46, 48,* 64, 72, *72–73*
  in South Dakota (1874), 76
Gompers, Samuel, 85
Goremykin, Ivan, *102*
Gorki, Maxim, *95*

Gorkiy (Nizhni Novgorod; USSR), *145*
Gosplan (State Planning Commission), 136, 138, *146*
government
  in American colonies, 29
  of Mayflower Compact, 21–22
  in post-Civil War American South, 76, 77
  Russian, during Revolution, 104, 110
  under US Constitution, 43–45
GPU (Soviet secret police), 145
Granovitaya Palace (Kremlin, Moscow), *135*
Grant, Ulysses S., 13, *69,* 75, 77
Grasse, Comte de, 41
Great American Tea Company, 46
Great Britain, *see* Britain
Great White Fleet, *86*
Greene, Nathanael, 41
Grenville, George, *18,* 31
Guadalupe Hidalgo, Treaty of (1848), 60
Guam, 88
Gulag (Labor Camp Administration), 146–148

Hamilton, Alexander, *34,* 45
Hampton Roads, battle of, *66*
Harper's Ferry (Virginia), John Brown's raid on, 65–68
Harrison, William Henry, 52
Hawaii, 13, 86, 88
Hawthorne, Nathaniel, 57
Hayes, Rutherford B., 80
Hearst, William Randolph, *81,* 86
Henry, Patrick, 32
Hickok, Wild Bill, 72
Hindenburg, Paul von, *109, 110*
Hitler, Adolf, 149–160, *165*
  World War Two propaganda of, 162, *162*
Hitler-Stalin Pact (1939), 153, *160*
Holland (Netherlands), 29
Homer, Winslow, *69*
Homestead Act (US, 1862), 81
Hooker, Thomas, 23
horses, 54
Houston, Sam, 60
Howe, William, 40
Hungary
  revolutionary socialist movement in, 121
  Soviet occupation of, 167, 168
Hutchinson, Anne, 23

Ignatiev, Nikolai, *102*
illiteracy, in Soviet Union, *125, 152*
immigration to US, 77, 82, *82–83,* 85
indentured servants, 21
Indians, American, 10, 18–23
  Apache, *76,* 81
  in battles with US, 75, 80–81
  Cherokee, 57
  after French and Indian War, 31
  Iroquois, *12, 17*
  Jefferson's treaties with, 35
  of Plains, 54, *54–55*
  railroads and, 59
  Seminole, *43*
  Seneca, *12*
  G. Washington and, 45
industrialization
  railroads and, 58–59
  in Russia, in 1890s, 105
  Soviet, electrification and, 138, *138–139*
  Soviet, after Lenin's death, 124–128
  Soviet, during World War Two, 153–160
  under Stalin, 136–137, *144–147,* 167
  in US, 14–15, 53–57, 81–85
Interstate Commerce Act (US, 1887), 84
Intolerable Acts (Coercive Acts; 1774), 35
inventions
  Edison's, 78, *78–79*
  in US, 53–57
Iroquois Indians, *12, 17*
Irving, Washington, 53
Isabella I (queen, Castile), 16
Iskra (The Spark; newspaper), 92, 95, *95*
Ivan IV (the Terrible; czar, Russia), *135, 159*
Ives, James M., *72*

Jackson, Andrew, *41, 42,* 52, 53, 57
James II (king, England), 23–29
Jamestown (Virginia), *13,* 19–21
Japan
  in Russo-Japanese War, *92, 96,* 97, *97,* 98, US and, *86,* 88
Jay, John, 41
Jay Treaty (1794), 45–48
Jefferson, Martha Wayles Skelton, *36*
Jefferson, Thomas, *34, 35,* 45, 64
  Declaration of Independence and, *29,* 40
  Indian treaties of, 35
  Louisiana Purchase and, 38, *39,* 48
  Monticello home of, 36, *36–37*
Johnson, Andrew, *64, 74,* 76–77
Joliet, Louis, *17*
Joseph (Nez Percé chief), 80

Kalinin, Mikhail, *151*
Kamenev, Lev, 120, 122, 128–131, 145, *156*
Kamenev, Sergei, *118*
Kansas, slavery issue in, 65
Kansas-Nebraska Act (US, 1854), 65
Kaplan, Dora, 116
Kearny, Stephen, 60
Keimer, Samuel, *25*
Kennesaw Mountain, battle of, *67*
Kerensky, Aleksandr, 88, 107, 109, *117, 121*
Kharkov (USSR), *126*
Khrushchev, Nikita, 160
Kipling, Rudyard, 13
Kirov, Sergei, *98,* 145, 157
kolkhozes (collective farms), *136–137,* 137–141
Kornilov, Lavr, 109
Kremlin (Moscow), *125, 134–135,* 135
  capture of (1917), *122*
Kronstadt (USSR), 116–118
Krupskaya, Nadezhda Konstantinovna, 90, 106, 107, 112, *112,* 124
Krylenko, Nikolai, *119*
Ku Klux Klan, 80
kulaks, 116, 119, *129,* 137, 141, 145
Kuznetsov, Pavel, *125*

labor unions
  in Soviet Union, *147*
  in US, 84–86
Lafayette, Marquis de, *18*
languages, spoken in USSR, 155
Latin America
  Monroe Doctrine and, 60
  T. Roosevelt's policy toward, 88
Latrobe, Benjamin H., *48*
Latvia, 153
Laurens, Henry, *43*
Lazarus, Emma, *10*
Lee, Robert E., 13, *69,* 75
Leisler, Jacob, 29
Lenin, Vladimir Ilyich (Ulyanov), 90–103, 105–112, *112–113,* 122, 135, 168
  on art, *150*
  attempted assassination of, 116
  on Bukharin, 128
  death of, 124, 131, *148*
  electrification plan of, 138, *138, 139*
  New Economic Policy of, 118–121
  purges of colleagues of, 145–146, 157
  Russian Revolution and, *95, 118,* 122, *123, 125*
  Trotsky and, 130
Leningrad (Petrograd; St. Petersburg; USSR), *91*
  revolution of 1905 in, 97–101, *100, 101*
  Revolution of 1917 in, 103–105, 109, *115–118, 122, 123, 125*
  Soviet capital moved to Moscow from, 135
Lewis, Meriwether, 38
Lexington, battle of, 35
Liberty Bell, *29*
Lincoln, Abraham, 60, *64,* 68–75, *68*
  assassination of, *74,* 76
Lincoln, Benjamin, 40
Lissitzky, El, *130, 150*
literature
  American, 53
  Soviet, Mayakovski and, *142, 142–143*

Lithuania, 153
Little Big Horn, battle of, *75*, 80
Livingston, Robert R., *29, 38*
Lone Star Republic (Texas), 60
Long Island, battle of, *30*
Lookout Mountain, battle of, *66*
Louisbourg (Canada), *16*, 31
Louisiana Territory
  given to Spain by Britain, 31
  slavery in, 60, 64
  US purchase of, 38, *39*, 48
Lowell, James Russell, 68
Lubyanka Prison (Moscow), *156*
Lunacharski, Anatoli, 150, *150*
Lvov, Georgi, 104, *115, 117*
Lvov, battles of, *110*

McClellan, George, *68*
Mcdonough, Thomas, *52*
Mackensen, August von, *109, 110*
McKinley, William, *85*, 86
Madison, James, *41*, 43, 48, 52, 57
Mahan, Alfred T., 86
Maine, 64
Maine (battleship), *84, 86*
Malevich, Kazimir, *150*
Malinovsky, Roman, 102
Manchuria, 92
Manila Bay, battle of, *85*, 88
Marquette, Père, *17*
Marx, Karl, 97, 120
Marxism, 127
Massachusetts, in American Revolution, 35–39
Massachusetts Bay colony, 22–29, 32
Massachusetts Spy (newspaper), *35*
Mayakovski, Vladimir, *139*, 142 *142–143*
Mayflower (ship), *15, 21*
Mayflower (steamboat), *64*
Mayflower Compact, 21–22
Mensheviks, 95–101, 107, 109, 116, 130
Mercer, Hugh, *31*
Mexico, wars between US and, *44*, 60
Minuit, Peter, *15*
Minutemen, *21*, 35
Missouri, slavery in, 60–64
Missouri Compromise (1820), 64
Molino del Rey, battle of, *44*
Monroe, James, 38, *42*, 57–60
Monroe Doctrine, 60, 88
Montana, 72, *73*
Montcalm, Marquis de, 31
Montgomery, Richard, 40
Montgomery Ward & Company, 46
Monticello (Virginia), 36, *36–37*
Montreal, battle of, *17*, 31
Morgan, John Pierpont, *81*, 84
Morris, Robert, 43
Moscow, *91*
  battle of, *166*
  Kremlin in, *125, 134–135*, 135
  Lenin's funeral in, *148*
  Lubyanka Prison in, *156*
  Red Square in, *130*
  Revolution of 1917 in, *122*
  Soviet capital moved to, 110, *123*
Mount Vernon (Virginia), *33*
Mucha, Alphonse, *129*
Munich (Germany), conference in (1938), 152, 153
Museum of the Revolution (Moscow), *148*

Napoleon Bonaparte (emperor, France), 38, 48, 52
Nashville, battle of, *67*
Natchez (Apache chief), *76*
National American Woman Suffrage Association, 86
National Association for the Advancement of Colored People (NAACP), 86
navy
  at Kronstadt, rebellion of, 116–118
  Russian, during Revolution, *121*
  in Russo-Japanese War, *96*
  Soviet, Stalin's purge of, 149

US, *84–86*, 86–88
Nazis, 149–160
  propaganda of, *162*
Netherlands (Holland), 29
New Economic Policy (NEP), 118–121, 124, 128, 138
New Hampshire, 23
New Mexico, 60, 64
New Orleans, battle of, *41*, 52
newspapers
  Russian, 114
  in US, *35*, 86
New York City, 50, *50–51*, 57
  in American Revolution, *30*, 40
  immigrants in, *82, 83*
  Statue of Liberty in, *10*
Nez Percé Indians, 80
Niagara Falls (US-Canada), *48*
Nicholas II (czar, Russia), *91*, *96*, 98, *101, 110*
  abdication of, *117*
Nicholas (grand duke, Russia), *108*
Nizhni Novgorod (Gorkiy; USSR), *145*
NKVD (Soviet secret police), 145
Nordica, Lillian Norton, *46*
North, Lord Frederick, 35, 41
Northwest Ordinance (US, 1787), 43, 60
Novosibirsk (Siberia), *156*

Ordzhonikidze, Grigori, *156*
Oregon, 60
Osceola (Seminole chief), *43*
Ottawa Indians, 31

Paine, Thomas, 9, 39
Palace of the Supreme Soviet (Kremlin, Moscow), *134*
Panama Canal, 88
Paris, Treaty of (1763), 31
Paris, Treaty of (1783), 41–43
Paris, Treaty of (1898), 88
Pasternak, Boris, 141–145, *142*
Paulus, Friedrich, *164–165*
Pea Ridge, battle of, *66*
peasants
  collective farms and, *136–137*, 137–140
  famine of 1920s and, *128–129*, 145
  in Russia, 116
  Soviet industrialization and, 124–128
  Soviet literacy campaigns for, *125*
Penn, Sir William *15*, 29
Pennsylvania, 29
Pennsylvania Gazette, 25, 30
Pequot Indians, 22–23
Perry, Oliver, 52
Peter I (the Great; czar, Russia), 135
Petersburg (Virginia), siege of, 75
Petrodvorets, recapture of, *166*
Petrograd, see Leningrad
Petrograd Soviet of Workers' and Soldiers' Deputies, 104, 107–110
Philadelphia (Pennsylvania), 40
Philip (Wampanoag chief), 23
Philippines, 13, *85*, 88
Pike, Zebulon M., 38
Pilgrims, *15, 21*
Pitt, William, 31
Platt Amendment (US, 1901), 88
Plymouth (Massachusetts), *15*, 21–22, 29
Poe, Edgar Allan, 53
Poland
  Soviet occupation of, 167, 168
  after World War One, *130*
  in World War Two, 153, *160*
political parties
  in post-Civil War US, 76
  in post-Revolutionary US, 45
Polk, James K., 60
Pontiac (Ottawa chief), 31
Populist Party (US), 84
Port Arthur (China), siege of, *96*
Portsmouth, Treaty of (1905), 97
Potemkin (battleship), *100*
Pravda (Truth, newspaper), 105, 128
Presnya (Russia), *99*

Princeton, battle of, *31*
Progressive movement (US), 86
Prokofiev, Sergei, *159*
Promontory Point (Utah), *59*, 80
propaganda, 162, *162–164*, 165
Provisional Government (Russia), 104, 107, 109, *115–117, 121*
Puerto Rico, 14, 86, 88
Pulitzer, Joseph, 86
Puritans, 9, 22

Quakers, 29
Quebec, battles of, *17*, 31, 40
Quebec Act (Britain, 1774), 35
Queenston Heights, battle of, *41*

Radek, Karl, *156*
railroads
  in Russia, pre-revolutionary, *105*
  Trans-Siberian, 92, 97
  Turkestan-Siberian, 147
  in US, 58–59, *59*, 80–84
Raleigh, Sir Walter, *13*
Rasputin, Grigori, *106*
Reconstruction (US South), 77–80
Red Army (USSR)
  Kronstadt rebellion suppressed by, 118
  in Russian civil war, *130*
  Stalin's purge of, 149
  under Trotsky, 114, *126, 127*
  Trotsky removed as head of, 131
  in World War Two, 157–167, *160–161, 163, 166*
Red Terror, 114–116
religion
  in American colonies, 21–29
  in Soviet Union, *141*
Republicans, post-Civil War, *74*, 76, 77
Reuterdahl, Henry, *86*
Revere, Paul, *18, 21*, 23
Rhode Island, 23
Ribbentrop, Joachim von, 153
Rochambeau, Comte de, 41
Rockefeller, John Davison, 81–84, *81*
Rodchenko, Aleksandr, *152*
Romania, 167, 168
Romanov dynasty (Russia), *91, 117*
Roosevelt, Franklin Delano, 167–168, *167*
Roosevelt, Theodore, 86, *86*, 88
Rozhdestvenski, Zinovi, *96*
Russia
  civil war in, 111–114, *130, 143*
  Lenin and, *112, 112–113*
  national minorities in, 121–122, 154–155
  revolution of 1905 in, 97–101, *98–102*
  in Russo-Japanese War, *92, 96, 97*
  in World War One, 102–103, *109*, 110–111, *110, 127*
  see also Soviet Union
Russian Revolution (1917), 88, 103–110, *115–117, 121*
  Bolshevik leadership in, *118–119*
  Lenin and *95, 113, 122, 123, 125*
  Trotsky and, 127
Russian Social-Democratic Workers' Party, 92–95, *95*
Russian Soviet Federated Socialist Republic (RSFSR), 154
  see also Soviet Union
Russo-Japanese War, *92*, 96, 97, *97*, 98
Rykov, Aleksei, *156*

St. Basil's Cathedral (Kremlin, Moscow), *135*
St. Petersburg, see Leningrad
San Francisco (California), *48*, 72
San Juan Hill, battle of, 86
Santa Anna, Antonio Lopez de, *44*
Santiago, battle of, 88
Saratoga, battle of, 40
Scott, Dred, 65
Scott, Winfield, *44*
Sedition Act (US, 1798), 48
Seminole Indians, 43
Seneca Indians, *12*
Seward, William H., 86

Shaw, Anna Howard, 86
Shays, Daniel, 43
Shepard, Thomas, 22
Sheridan, Philip H., *68,* 75
Sherman, William Tecumseh, 75
Sherman Antitrust Act (US, 1890), 84
Shiloh, battle of, *67*
shipping
  Embargo Act and, 48
  in New York City, *50, 51,* 57
  War of 1812 and, 52
Sioux Indians, *54–55, 75, 76,* 80
Sitting Bull (Sioux chief), *75*
slavery and slaves, 10–12, 61
  in American colonies, 21
  cotton gin and, 57
  Emancipation Proclamation and, *64,* 69
  Thirteenth Amendment abolition of, 75
  in US territories, 60–65
Smith, John, 20
Smolny Institute (Leningrad), *117, 122, 123, 125*
Socialist Realism, *150*
society
  in American colonies, 21
  Soviet, nationalities in, 121–122, 143–155
  Soviet, peasants in, 124–128
  US, urbanization of, 85–86
Solzhenitsyn, Aleksandr, 148
Sons of Liberty, *20,* 32, 35
South Dakota, 72, *76,* 77
Soviet Union (USSR; Russia)
  art of, 150, *150–151*
  Eisenstein and, 158, *158–159*
  electrification in, 138, *138–139*
  Kronstadt rebellion in, 116–118
  Lenin and, 112, *112–113*
  after Lenin's death, 124–136, *149*
  Mayakovski and, 142, *142–143*
  national minorities in, 121–122, 154–155
  New Economic Policy in, 118–121
  seal of, *90*
  under Stalin, 136–153, *146*
  Stalinist purges in, *156,* 157
  Trotsky and, *126–127,* 127
  in World War Two, 153–167, *160–161, 166*
  after World War Two, 168
  World War Two propaganda and, 162, *162–164*
  see also Russia; Russian Revolution
sovkhozes (state farms), 140–141
Spain
  Florida sold to US by, *42,* 57
  horses introduced into North America by, 54
  Louisiana under, 31
  New World exploration by, 16
  in Spanish-American War, *84, 85,* 86–88
Spanish-American War, *84, 85,* 86–88
Spencer, Herbert, 84
Stakhanov, Alexei, 136–137
Stalin, Joseph (Dzhugashvili), *90, 97, 109, 119, 162*
  art under, 150, *150*
  as commissar for nationalities, 110, 121–122
  as Communist Party general secretary, 122–124
  dispute between Trotsky and, 128–136, *149*
  Eisenstein and, 158, *159*
  foreign policies of, 149–153
  Kirov and, *98*
  pact between Hitler and, *160*
  purges under, 145–149, *156,* 157
  during Revolution of 1917, 104–105, *121*
  pre-Revolutionary background of, 101–102
  Soviet Union under, 136–145, *146*
  during World War Two, 153–167, *166*
  after World War Two, 167–168
  World War Two propaganda of, 162
  at Yalta conference, *167*
Stalingrad, battle of, *164–166,* 167
Stamp Act (1765), *18,* 32
Standard Oil Corporation, *81,* 84
Stanford, Leland, *59*
Stanton, Edwin M., 77
Statue of Liberty (New York), *10*
Stevens, Thaddeus, 76
Stieglitz, Alfred, *83*

Stolypin, Pëtr, *102*
Strong, Josiah, 86
Stuyvesant, Peter, *15,* 29
Sugar Act (1764), 32
Sullivan, Sir Arthur, 78
Sully, Thomas, *37*
Sumner, Charles, 65, 76
Sunni Moslems, 121
Sverdlov, Yakov, 119

Taft, William H., 86
Talleyrand-Périgord, Charles Maurice de, 38
Taney, Roger B., 65
taxes
  imposed on colonies by Britain, *18,* 32, 35
  in post-Revolutionary US, 45
Taylor, Zachary, 60
Tea Act (1773), *20,* 35
Tecumseh (Indian chief), *39,* 52
Teheran (Iran), conference at (1943), 167–168
Tenure of Office Act (US, 1867), 76
Texas, in Mexican War, *44,* 60
Thames, battle of the, *39*
Tilden, Samuel J., 80
Tippecanoe, battle of, 52
tobacco, *13,* 20, 21, *46*
Tocqueville, Alexis de, 14
Togo, Heihachiro, *96*
Tolstoi, Lev, *107*
Toussaint L'Ouverture, Pierre Dominique, 48
Townshend duties (1767), 32
trade, *see* commerce
Trans-Siberian Railroad, *92, 97*
Trenton, battle of, *30*
Trepov, Dmitri, *102*
Trist, Nicholas P., 60
Trollope, Frances, *51*
Trotsky, Leon, 122, *126–127, 127,* 135, 168
  on art, 150
  dispute between Stalin and, 102, 123, 128–136, 145, 148, *149,* 157, 167
  Kronstadt rebellion suppressed by, 118
  murder of, 146
  on peasantry and agriculture, 124–128, 137
  Red Army under, 114
  before revolution of 1905, 89–92, 95–97
  in revolution of 1905, 97–101
  in Revolution of 1917, 105, 107–110
Tsaritsyn (Volgograd; USSR), *126*
Tsushima, battle of, *96*
Tubman, Harriet, *61*
Tukhachevski, Mikhail, *156*
Turkestan-Siberian Railway, *147*
Twain, Mark, 72

Ulyanov, Alexander, 92, *112*
Ulyanov, Vladimir Ilyich, *see* Lenin, Vladimir Ilyich
underground railroad, 64
Union (North in US Civil War), 69, 75
Union Pacific Railroad, 59, *59,* 80
Union of Soviet Socialist Republics (USSR), *see* Soviet Union
United States (US)
  advertising in, 46, *46*
  Civil War in, *64, 66–67,* 69–76
  Constitution of, 44–45
  early settlements of, 16–21
  Edison and, 78, *78–79*
  Franklin and, 24
  during Great Depression, 137
  immigrants in, 82, *82–83*
  industrialization of, 81–85
  Jefferson and, 36, *36*
  Louisiana Purchase and, 38
  in Mexican War, *44,* 60
  New York City and, 50, *50–51*
  Plains Indians of, 54, *54–55*
  railroads in, 58–59, *59*
  in Russian civil war, 114
  in Spanish-American War, *84, 85,* 86–88
  in War of 1812, *41,* 52
  in war with France (1798), 48

see also America; American Revolution
United States Steel Corporation, *81,* 84
Uritski, Moisei, *118*

Valley Forge (Pennsylvania), *30,* 40
Vanderbilt, Cornelius, *81*
Veblen, Thorstein, 46
Vicksburg, battle of, *67*
Virginia, 32
Virginia Company of London, 19–21
Vladimirov, Ivan, *98*
Vladivostok (USSR), *92*
Volgograd (Tsaritsyn; USSR), *126*
Voroshilov, Kliment, *119*
Vyshinsky, Andrei, *156*

Wald, Lillian, *82*
Wampanoag Indians, 23
War Communism, 116, 118, *140*
wars
  American Revolution, 21–23, 29–31, 32–41
  between American settlers and Indians, 19
  between Britain and Holland, 29
  civil (Russia), 111–114, *126, 130, 143*
  Civil (US), 13, *64, 66–67,* 69–76
  of 1812, *41,* 52
  between France and US, 48
  French and Indian, *16, 17,* 30–31
  French Revolution, 45
  Mexican, *44,* 60
  Russo-Japanese, *92, 96, 97, 97,* 98
  Spanish-American, *84, 85,* 86–88
  World War One, 88, 102–104, 107, *108, 109,* 110–111, *110,* 127
  World War Two, 157–167, *160–166*
  see also individual battles
Washington, Booker T., 86
Washington, George
  in American Revolution, *18,* 23, *30, 31,* 38, 40, 41
  in French and Indian War, 30
  as president, *32, 33,* 45, 50
Washington, John Augustine, 30
Washington, Martha, *33*
Washington (District of Columbia)
  Capitol building of, *48*
  in War of 1812, *41,* 52
Waugh, S., *83*
Weems, Mason, 57
Wehrmacht (German armed forces), 160, *161*
Wells, H. G., *82*
White (Russian) armies, 111–114, *126, 130, 143*
Whitman, Walt, 10, 12
Whitney, Eli, 53, 57
Wilderness Campaign (US Civil War), 75
William II (kaiser, Germany), *109*
Williams, Roger, 23
Williamsburg (Virginia), battle of, *67*
Wilson, Woodrow, 86, 88
Winter Palace (Leningrad), 109, *121*
Winthrop, John, 22, 23
Wolfe, James, *17,* 31
women
  in abolitionist movement, 64
  in Jamestown colony, 20–21
  suffrage for, in US, 86
Women's Rights Convention (Seneca Falls, 1848), 64–65
World War One, 88
  British propaganda in, 162
  czarist forces in, *108, 110*
  Germany in, *109*
  Lenin on, 102–103
  Russian Provisional Government in, 104, 107
  Treaty of Brest Litovsk and, 110–111, *127*
World War Two, 153–167, *160–166*
Wounded Knee, massacre of, 80
Wrangel, Pëtr, *130*

Yalta (USSR), conference at (1945), *167,* 168
Yorktown, battle of, *31,* 40, 41

Zhukov, Georgi, *166*
Zinoviev, Grigori, 116, *119,* 128–131, 145, *156*